PASSION PURPOSE PROTECTION

The *Ability* of Disability Insurance

JOHN F. NICHOLS MSN, CLU

For more information:
www.drg.com/ppp
800-945-9719

ISBN: 978-0-692-26823-0 / paperback
ISBN: 978-0-692-26824-7 / hardcover
ISBN: 978-0-692-26825-4 / eBook

~

To those valiantly overcoming adversity
and living one step at a time
to achieve their DAILY VICTORY!
You inspire me to capture my dreams and goals.

To my parents, siblings,
my industry peers, business associates,
friends and supporters
—let's distribute this book
to all those you know who rely
on their abilities to earn an income.

CONTENTS

FOREWORD

Author's Story: Life Happens... the Direction Is Your Choice

WISH YOU COULD have been there.

It was a little before seven a.m. on Sunday, October 11, 2009. A chilly thirty-four-degrees-Fahrenheit wind was blowing across Lake Michigan as the sun started to rise. Forty-five thousand people had signed up for the Chicago Marathon, but only thirty-five thousand actually showed up.

Over the loudspeaker came the announcement: "Thirty seconds!"

We started pulling off our runner warm-ups and tossing them to the side of the road.

Three...

Two...

One...

BANG!

The Chicago Marathon starting line

The starter's gun sounded and we started moving forward on our journey. The first two miles were a blur—I was lost in the excitement. My adrenaline was pumping; the huge crowds were cheering. Over the loudspeakers, Bono from the band U2 was singing: "It's a beautiful day, don't let it get away."

As I turned my focus to the other runners around me, I saw Becki, who was the pace leader for the five hour, thirty minutes group. I'd met her the night before at the runners' pasta party, where I had told everyone I wouldn't be running due to a right knee injury. So when Becki saw me, she was quite surprised. "John, I thought you weren't running."

"Well, I changed my mind." My *cause* was too important; my *desire* was burning; the *opportunity* was present, right here, right now; my *commitment* was hanging heavy over my head and heart. I had *persisted* through sixteen grueling weeks of training before my knee injury and I wanted my personal *victory*. You see, I was running for Danielle. I was trying to raise $26,000 for our common cause—$1,000 for every mile I completed.

"Becki, can I join your group?" I asked.

Becki gave me a huge grin. "Absolutely, John. Let's kick butt!"

For the next twelve miles I ran with Becki's group, first heading north for five miles toward Wrigley Field, home of the Chicago Cubs baseball team, then turning back south toward downtown, then out west as we made our way toward the United Center, home of the Chicago Bulls basketball and Blackhawks hockey teams.

As we were approaching mile fourteen, my right knee buckled, then gave out entirely. I stumbled, then fell to the ground. I got back to my feet slowly, only to see Becki and the pace group pulling away. Then, looking toward the side of the road, there were the excuses—school buses with large signs painted in pink neon: DROPOUT RUNNERS.

The excuse bus

No, no, not me, I thought. *I've come too far.*

For the next five miles, I shuffled a half mile, then speed walked the other half. Shuffled a half, speed walked half.

By mile nineteen, my right knee and leg were pleading with me, *No more, please no more. I can't take the pain anymore.*

Those dropout school buses showed up again. Almost as though they were following me, begging me to give up. You know all the excuses: you can't finish, your leg hurts. You could always say you will try again next year. Everyone will understand.

I screamed, "I have to finish. I made a commitment. I have to make it official."

At mile 19. Not done yet.

In order to do so, I would have to finish within six hours, thirty minutes. I had seven miles and three hundred and eighty-five yards to go. I quickly calculated that I would have to average about one mile every fifteen minutes to meet my goal. So I pushed on—speed walking as fast as I could, dragging my right leg along. Mile twenty…twenty-one…twenty-two…

The winner of the 2009 Chicago Marathon finished in two hours, five minutes, and forty-one seconds. The average marathoner finished in four hours, ten minutes. Out of the thirty-five thousand runners I was the thirty-two thousand, three hundred and sixth runner to cross the finish line, with a time of six hours, nine minutes, and fifty-nine seconds. Officially finishing, fulfilling my commitment and celebrating my victory—and I have the medal to prove it!

Not bad for a recovering C5-C6 incomplete quadriplegic.

Official Marathon finisher!

Career Beginnings

Let's go back in time to the year 1992. I was a struggling insurance advisor, in my eighth year in the business and on my second employer, located in a new city, Chicago, Illinois. Around this time, an insurance professional from my hometown in Minnesota approached me to discuss an opportunity. Rita and I had met through our industry's association events. After a few meetings, we decided to form a partnership in which I would secure an HIV/disability product for her client (the US accrediting body for all the medical schools) and she would manage the client relationships. We went to market in 1993, and by July we had signed up thirty-eight of the sixty medical schools in the United States. We became one of the country's largest providers of HIV/disability programs for medical students.

As you can imagine, as a young man—just thirty-two—I was on top of the world. I made more money than I ever could have envisioned and I was living accordingly. I purchased a sweet bachelor pad, a hot-looking—and fast—Porsche 911, and the clothes to match. I was living the life—at least from the outside in.

It was the last weekend of July 1993, and my buddies and I were off to our annual party weekend at Dave's lake cabin in northern Wisconsin. After playing a round of golf on Friday morning, we headed back to the cabin to hang out on the lake.

My buddy Dan headed into the cabin to grab the cooler of beer and soft drinks while Rich and Sheila launched the speedboat and prepared it for the waterskiing runs.

I was first up on the skis, so I made my way down to the dock. As I was walking across, I picked up a life preserver and a pair of skis. I slipped on my life jacket and zipped it up. Sitting on the edge of the dock, I let my legs dangle into the cool and calm water. I grabbed a ski and pulled it onto my left foot, then pulled on the ski for my right foot. Because the lake was so placid, we were able to do a dock start. Rich maneuvered the boat out in front of me, slowly inching forward toward the open water; Sheila threw me the ski rope and the handle splashed down in front of me. They waited for my signal.

I grabbed the rope handle that lay in the water and as my arm came up, I gave Rich the thumbs-up signal and yelled, "Hit it!"

Rich slammed on the accelerator and the boat screamed ahead. Just then, I looked down and noticed some slack in the line. I had to let go for my own safety, but it was too late—I couldn't drop the handle fast enough.

The boat surged across the lake; the ski rope abruptly knotted and pulled taut. The force pulled me into the air. Almost immediately I came crashing down headfirst. Unfortunately, the lake was only about four feet deep right there at the edge of the dock. My head sliced through the water and hit the lake's bottom—hard.

Amazingly, I remained conscious, though I was stunned. It seemed to me that time had slowed and thickened, like the water all around me. As I floated upward, I knew I had to get my head above the surface; I had to call out for help. Did my friends even realize what had happened? Was it possible they were still motoring happily across the lake, completely oblivious?

My life vest ensured that I made it to the surface, but once there, my chin lay against my chest while my arms floated out uselessly. I was able to look around for help, but there was nothing but water. Oddly enough, I wasn't afraid just then. I could see the bubbles escaping from my mouth; I was looking around for help but couldn't do anything for myself. It was surreal. The whole world was silent, peaceful…so beautiful.

As I floated there, my mind was moving in overdrive. Images flickered through my mind: my childhood. My parents. My brothers and sisters. Playing basketball with my friends.

What little breath I could get was coming fast now. I knew, on some level, that these were the last breaths I would ever take. But at the same time, everything was so dark and so quiet. I was just floating. It felt, in that moment, like it was more than water holding me up. I felt myself drifting away. Ahead there was light and the shadows of people.

It seemed as though they were reaching out to welcome me, but I never made it.

When I remember this moment, this moment when I knew I was about to die, I do not recall terror or sadness. I remember only that warm feeling and the ease of floating away. That day I learned that death was not to be feared. I learned, too, that there were things a whole lot worse than dying.

Dying is so peaceful and loving. Be not afraid.

Becoming disabled is a living nightmare. Be afraid.

Rescue or Divine Intervention?

Many stories have a hero and Dan Gardner was mine—he gave me a second chance to live again. At the time of my "funny fall," Dan was walking with the cooler down the hill toward the beach. He could hear the music from the Depeche Mode CD playing over the outdoor speakers, and at first he chuckled when he saw me splash into the lake. He laughed even more when he saw my body flopping around, seemingly harmlessly. As he drew closer to the shore, however, it became clear to Dan that something was terribly wrong. It was taking me way too long to reach above the surface. All Dan saw was my body floating helplessly away.

Immediately, Dan stripped down to his shorts and swam fifty yards to my body. He gave me a push and I bobbed like a buoy—I was already unconscious. With his left hand Dan clutched my life preserver and turned my head and body toward him. He saw blood gushing down my face from a head wound. Then, looking into my eyes, he only saw the whites, as my eyes had rolled back into my head. My life was coming to an end and Dan was holding onto my corpse.

As Dan held onto me, he started swimming back to shore. He reached the dock to catch his breath and yelled at me, "John, wake up, wake up!" No response. Dan started swimming again and dragged me along, all the way to the shoreline, where he laid out my limp body.

As fate would have it, Dan had learned how to perform CPR just a month earlier. He immediately began chest compressions and water burbled out of my nose and mouth.

The first thing I remember after regaining consciousness was Dan's panicky voice: "John, John, what can you feel? What can you feel?"

Still in a state of shock, I mumbled something about a pain in my upper right shoulder. Neither of us realized the extent of my injuries. By this time, Rich had parked the boat at the dock and Sheila ran up to the cabin to call for an ambulance.

Twenty minutes later—an eternity to my friends who were standing around in a somber mood—the ambulance arrived. The paramedics jumped out and grabbed their equipment and the stretcher. After assessing the situation, they put a head and neck brace on me and gave me a shot of steroids. They called over a few of the guys and asked for their assistance in pulling the body board through the sand so as to move my body as little as possible. Once the board was in place, they secured my body, neck, and head with straps from one side of the body board to the other. Then on a count of three, *one-two-three*, they lifted me up and onto a stretcher and pushed me into the ambulance.

The ambulance raced off to the nearest hospital with a few of my friends following behind in their cars. Dan stayed behind at the cabin. With no one around to see him, he went behind the beach shed and wept uncontrollably. The music played on. It was the Depeche Mode song that played on and still haunts Dan to this day.

You had something to hide
Should have hidden it, shouldn't you
Now you're not satisfied
With what you're being put through
It's just time to pay the price
For not listening to advice
And deciding in your youth
On the policy of truth.
—"Policy of Truth," Depeche Mode

The ambulance transported me to the small hospital in town, where the staff was only able to stabilize me. Morphine became my best friend as it suspended reality and eased the pain. After about three hours, they loaded me into another ambulance and drove me to a larger hospital near Wausau, Wisconsin. Wausau Medical Center had one neurosurgeon on staff. He performed the operation to affix my new headgear—a halo—to hold my neck in place and prevent any further damage to the spinal cord.

The next morning when I woke up, an older gentleman was sitting at my bedside. "Son," he said, "my name is Dr. Moran. I am the neurosurgeon on staff at this hospital. I have good news and bad news. The good news is that you will live. You are in critical but stable condition. The bad news is that your injury will create a different and difficult life ahead for you. You have suffered a broken neck. Your vertebrae were fractured and broken. There was also a dislodging of the discs between the vertebrae. These two conditions caused tearing, punctures, and a large contusion to the spinal cord. We have diagnosed you as an incomplete C5-C6 quadriplegic. John, my thoughts and prayers are with you."

Dr. Moran retired the next day and I never saw him again.

The spinal cord is, as the name implies, a cord approximately one-quarter- to one-half-inch thick, and it is tragically vulnerable to the type of injuries that I had suffered. The vertebral column surrounding the spinal cord is intended to support and protect. But if the individual vertebrae are broken and disrupted, not only is the spine unprotected, but the jagged vertebrae themselves can cut, puncture, or fray the spinal cord.

And the consequences are serious indeed. The spinal cord's job is to transmit neural signals from the brain to various parts of the body. These neural signals do everything from telling your muscles to move your body around to telling your bladder to empty. It controls how we feel pain, how we breathe—almost everything about what it means to be alive that we take for granted.

Every spinal cord injury is a bit different and leaves the sufferer with different capabilities or lack thereof. In my case, I had no controlled movements from my neck all the way down to my toes, and that included control of my bowel and bladder movements. In a brief moment of life, the time it took for a boat to rev up, for me to fall a little more than five feet, I had gone from a healthy, vibrant person in the prime of my life to a nonfunctioning quadriplegic.

CHAPTER 1

I Didn't Know What I Didn't Know — Do You?

NO ONE REALLY wants to think about becoming disabled, in the same way that no one wants to think about a tornado blowing their home away, a house fire, or even an automobile accident. No one wants to imagine all the bad things that could happen to them. So, for the most part, we don't. We take each day as it comes, imagining that tomorrow will proceed in the same way. After all, we are invincible, aren't we?

When I went up to the cabin that weekend, I didn't imagine for a second that I could come home a quadriplegic. A catastrophic accident or illness happened to other people, not to me! We go about our daily lives full of hopes, dreams, and optimism for the future and then a rude awakening happens. As I lay in my hospital bed, I questioned if I was prepared enough. Could anyone ever really be prepared for this? What was my plan B, my backup plan? What would I do now?

The seriousness of my medical condition and the retirement of Dr. Moran meant that I would need another hospital to continue my medical care. A decision was made to admit me to Froedtert Memorial Hospital in Milwaukee. On Sunday morning, they packed me up, put me into an ambulance, drove me to the Wausau airport, and flew me in an air ambulance to Milwaukee. After another ambulance ride, I arrived at Froedtert Memorial Hospital, which became my new home.

Three days had passed and I'd been in four hospitals and as many ambulances, and probably a hundred people had touched my body in one way or another. I felt exposed and picked over. Everything was out of my control. Even the smallest, most ordinary tasks required me to depend on someone else. On top of being unable to dress myself or use the bathroom, I couldn't even dial a phone. Everything required someone else's assistance. I couldn't even sign my own name and instead marked an unsteady X as my signature. Before I could get any sort of treatment, the doctors had to witness me slowly, with assistance, marking my X on the hospital paperwork.

To suddenly be disabled is to experience a whole new level of helplessness. And this is coming from someone who made a living selling disability insurance! Now I needed it. How crazy ironic is that?

There I was, lying in my bed, alone. The halo was bulky and awkward, and I was never comfortable, which made sleeping more difficult. I spent those days on my back with no movement. Where everything had seemed accelerated in the previous days, now the hours and minutes stretched out, slow as molasses. The brain was on, the body wasn't. The thinking would not stop.

I knew by then how serious my condition was. Or rather, I had been told how serious my condition was. I still couldn't help feeling disconnected from the reality of the situation. It was too much, too big. My brain threw up walls to ward it off and reduce it to a more manageable scale. *This has to be a dream*, I thought. *Is this a dream?*

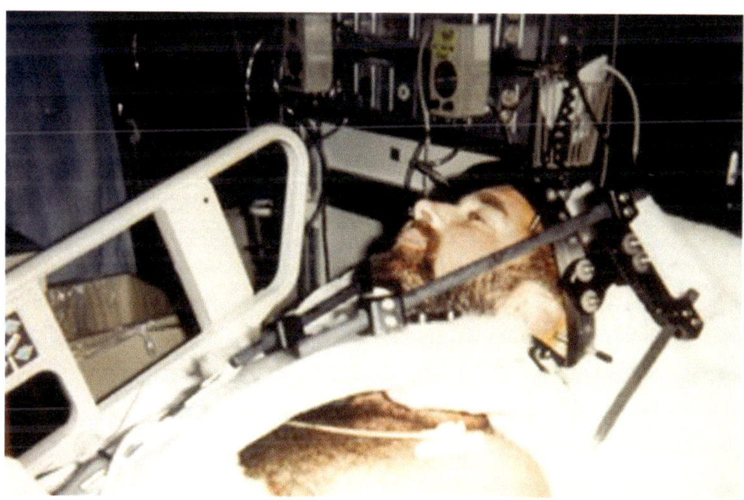

Tell me this is a dream.

My body had changed in an instant. The circumstances of my life had changed overnight. But people can't change that fast. Before I fell off that dock, I was a hard-driving, independent, athletic go-getter. There was no way that I was going to let someone take over my life. I wasn't going to leave my fate in the hands of others. I wasn't going to let them tell me what I could or couldn't do. I had faith in myself. I'd always overcome the naysayers before, so why should I listen to them now?

Of course, my fate was, in many ways, out of my hands. Even as I lay there wondering if this was a dream, the doctors and my parents were working to develop a medical plan of action. I would need surgery to repair and remove the broken vertebrae and disc. The problem was, the damaged disc was in an awkward spot. The surgeon would have to go through

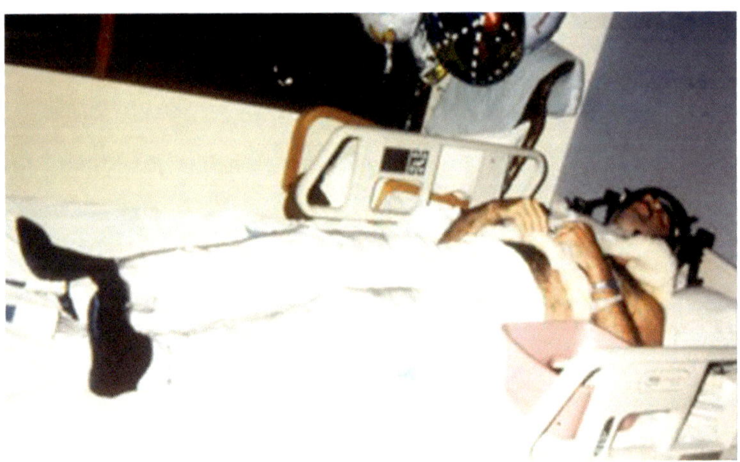

Brain working, body NOT

both the front and back of my neck to remove it. The alternate option was to just tie the disc down using a piece of bone from my hip. In that case, they would only need to go through the back of my neck. The downside was that, even tied down, the broken disc would partially impede my airway and possibly obstruct swallowing.

Dr. Namme, the primary neurosurgeon, recommended removing the disc. My parents wanted a second opinion. Fortunately, Dr. Namme checked his ego at the door, as he wanted all parties involved to agree upon the plan of action before moving forward. After the second opinion came in, there was some discussion and, ultimately, the decision was made to go with plan B.

Before they could move forward with the surgery, the swelling around the injured area would have to go down. It was during this time that we first learned about an experimental drug for spinal cord injuries that was being tested at the very hospital where I was being treated. The drug proposed to stimulate the recovery of nerves and might help me regain some voluntary motion. Because of the extent of my injury and my prognosis, I was a good candidate for the study. The protocol was simple: I would be administered the drug and/or a placebo every day for the next thirty days. At some point in the future, they would "unblind" the test and the results would be revealed.

It was an amazing opportunity; my family and I clung to it like a life preserver. But my sole focus at the time was getting back to work. As far as I was concerned, becoming a quadriplegic was just a mere road bump. At the very least, I was trying hard to make it into one. I had a closing appointment with a large entity with five thousand participants in two weeks. This was a once-in-a-lifetime, career-making opportunity to sell my disability program. It was a $1 million sale! Even though my life had been completely turned upside down, in that moment all I could think about was that meeting and how I could not, under any circumstances, miss it.

My reaction was hardly unusual. Dr. Namme and the medical staff often dealt with patients who could not initially accept the realities of their situation. They had a number of medical and psychological tactics designed to prepare me for my new reality of life in a wheelchair. But my resistance—and my denial—were strong.

Dr. Namme sent my parents, my peers, my friends, even a priest to visit me, all in an attempt to get me to start accepting my new life. But I wasn't hearing any of it. I had built a mental wall around myself so thick that nothing and nobody was going to penetrate it.

It wasn't that I was stupid—just stubborn to the core. No one knew me better than I knew myself and I knew that I was

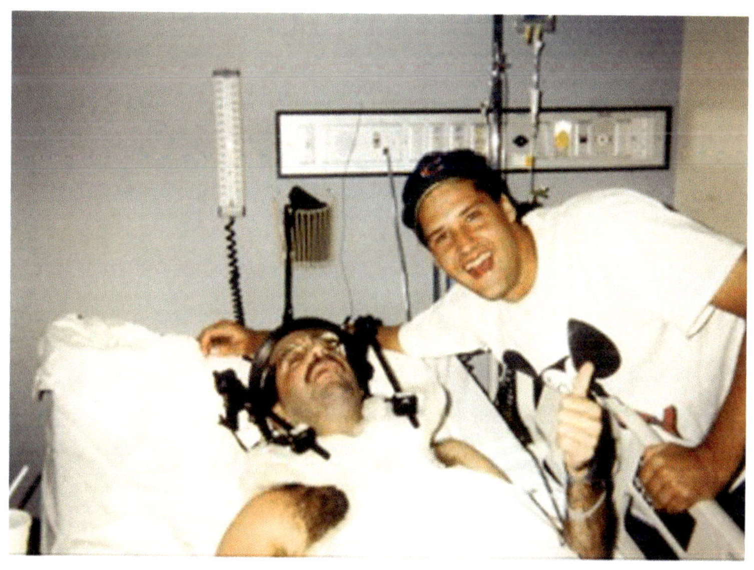

Thumbs up - not really!

going to get my life back. I knew I was not going to rely on my family, friends, or relatives to wash me or help me use the toilet.

The fact of the matter was, I was staring down the barrel of an existence that was short on independence and even shorter on dignity and I was doing everything I could to hold on to my sense of self-worth and dignity as long as I could. In my mind, the business appointment and million-dollar sale took on mythic status. If I could just get to this meeting, if I could just pull this off, it would be an unmistakable sign that everything was going to be okay. That I was going to be okay and someday everything would be just like it was before.

While my attitude was understandable, it was hardly helpful, and Dr. Namme was getting a little fed up with me. One day he stopped by my hospital room and we had a heart-to-heart visit.

"John, what's it going to take to have you start accepting our medical advice and care?"

"Well, Dr. Namme," I told him, "I have this upcoming appointment that I can't miss. It's too important. I'm in the running for this huge sale. Career-making huge. I have to be at this meeting."

The doctor looked thoughtful for a moment. "I see," he said. "How about you and I make a deal: I'll let you go on the appointment if you can show me some improvement."

That sounded incredibly reasonable to me. I was sure to demonstrate some solid improvement soon. After all, this was just a temporary setback!

"Okay," I said, glad that it seemed someone was finally recognizing how important this meeting really was.

Dr. Namme looked sternly into my eyes. "However, John, if there is no improvement, you must start accepting our medical care and begin to learn the activities of daily living."

That sounded like a cinch to me. "I'm all in, Dr. Namme." I grinned. "What do you want me to do?"

Dr. Namme called in my rehabilitation team, Jim and Mary. They transferred me into a wheelchair and rolled me down to the rehabilitation room. My parents, the nurses, and other patients were in the room as well.

I was glad to have an audience, because this was my big day and I was going to show them all that my life wasn't over, that I was still the same person. Jim and Mary rolled me over to the parallel bars; they each grabbed a side of me and pulled me up to the bars. They placed my hands on the bars and inched away from me.

There I stood, watching everyone watch me. It felt like hours, days, but it was probably only about a minute or so. My arms started to shake and then my legs. My body began to give out. Suddenly, tears streamed down my face. My brain screamed for my body to move, just a footstep, just an inch. But there was nothing. My brain, so convinced that I was going to pull through all this right away, had no power whatsoever over my rebellious body.

Jim and Mary caught me as I slumped back down into the wheelchair. For the first time, I realized just how little control I had, not just over my circumstances, but over my own body. From my chin to my toes, nothing! No movement. And that realization crushed me. They had finally broken me.

Once the swelling went down, I was scheduled for surgery to repair and remove the broken vertebrae as well as tie down the disc. There was no surgery that could fix the damage to my spinal cord—and there still isn't.

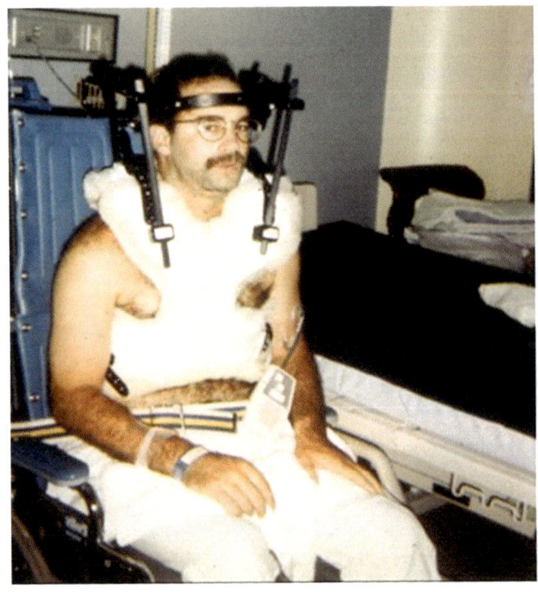

@#%! Not Happy

After the procedure, back in my hospital room, Dr. Namme provided a summary for me: "John, the surgery went well. However, your injury is very serious. The spinal cord is damaged in a number of areas; there is a tear and a couple of punctures from the bone fragments. I can't make any predictions. I can only hope the best for you."

After the surgery, Dr. Namme's job was done. He put me in the hands of the rehabilitation team and offered me the claims forms for Social Security disability benefits as well as for my own private disability insurance plans.

The first step in my recovery was to learn the ADLs (activities for daily living). These are basic living tasks, consisting of:

- Personal hygiene
- Dressing and undressing
- Eating
- Moving from bed to chair and back (as opposed to being bedridden)
- Voluntarily/involuntary control of urinary and fecal discharge.

Jim and Mary met with me to discuss my specific rehabilitation plan: Jim would work with me on bigger movements, while Mary would focus on the internal issues and smaller functions. The rehabilitation team starts slowly, training you on the first of these tasks and then evaluating your level of ability before determining the next course of action.

At the same time, there would be a series of meetings with the social workers who help patients and families with state services and home modifications. My mom was particularly interested in these meetings, as she was planning to move me back to Minnesota with her and my father. My worst nightmare was coming true—not just living with my parents, but being dependent on them as well. I would be humbled each and every day for the rest of my life.

But even in the face of that depressing prospect, there were reasons to hope. Years later, my father would say that he'd witnessed two miracles in his life. The first was when I lived through the accident and near drowning that should have killed me. The second was the moment when my left toes started wiggling.

This happened about a week or so after the surgery. It was like a shaft of sunlight in a dark room. Almost immediately, I started thinking about my rehabilitation program and how much of my physical capability I could realistically get back. I would have worked round-the-clock if they had let me—and if I had been able.

Unfortunately, my brain was still moving a lot faster than my body. Jim would show up for our eight a.m. rehabilitation session and find me snoring away in my bed. Mentally and physically, I was exhausted all the time.

For every week in bed with no movement, the body loses approximately 20 percent of its muscle, as well the attendant muscle memory. After four weeks, I had lost between 60 and 70 percent of my muscle mass and muscle memory.

"Let's get to work!" Jim said, lifting me up to the bars and holding me as steady as he could. My body would shake, just like that first time. My arms would start to give out. *I can do it, I can do it,* I kept telling myself, like a mantra. And then one day, there was a twitch—really more like a flinch of movement—from the left leg. It wasn't much, just a few inches. It caught both of us off guard and we chuckled—a sigh of relief and joy. Jim helped me back into the wheelchair. We looked at each other and said, "Baby steps!"

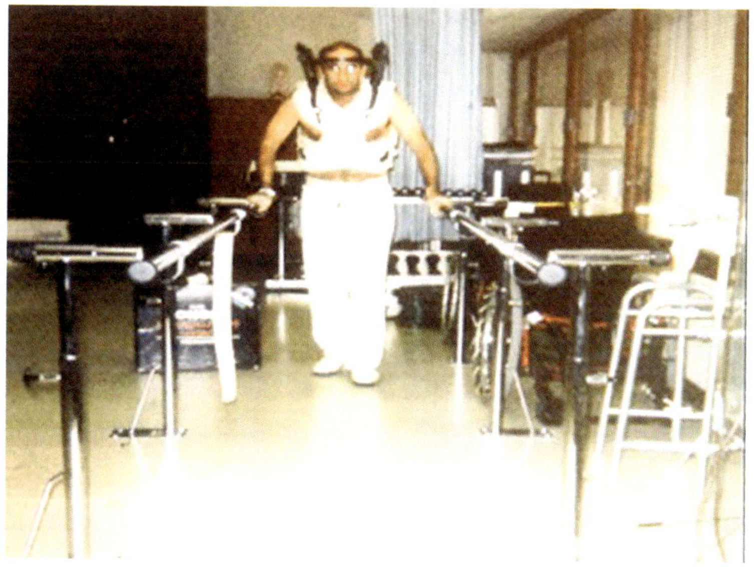

First baby steps

I learned to find daily victories in even the smallest progress. It took about a week before I could inch my way down the length of the parallel bars. The right side of my body always lagged a couple of weeks behind my left side. Once I accomplished one length of the parallel bars, we moved on to a full lap. Mind you, the length of those parallel bars was a whopping ten feet!

It wasn't pretty by any means, but Jim was always right there to catch me. From the parallel bars to the grandma walker to double canes, it would take years, but I was relearning how to walk. Well, at least how to shuffle my way forward. Even with so much effort and rehabilitation, I still struggled and my right side and foot always lagged behind.

There were just so many things: the tiniest everyday functions I had taken for granted. Mary, my occupational therapist, worked with me endlessly as I relearned how to shave my face, comb my hair, button my buttons, and tie my shoes. These are tasks we learn at such an early age that it's hard for us to even imagine a life in which we are incapable of them. Mary even used electrical-shock therapy to try wake up the nerves to fire the muscles. Just saying it brings back the pain! Ouch.

Imagine all the things you couldn't do if you lost your ability, strength, or dexterity: button your shirt, tie your shoes, bathe and shave, eat, walk, make phone calls. The list goes on and on…

My release date from Froedtert Memorial Hospital was coming up, and there were still a few big issues to resolve. First, did I have the ability to take care of myself—was I independent

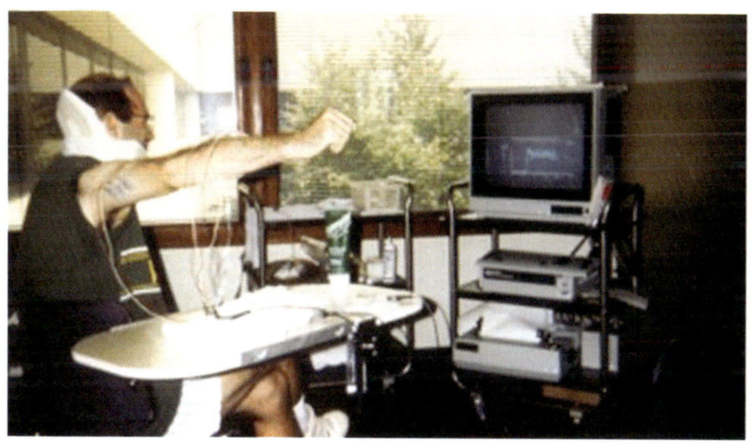

Electrical shock therapy - ouch!

or dependent? Secondly, where was I going to go? Back to my sweet bachelor pad in Chicago, or to Minnesota to live with Mommy and Daddy?

I would have done just about anything to avoid the latter. And my parents, though they loved me and were prepared to do whatever I needed, probably weren't thrilled about the prospect either. They had raised their children to be independent and did not expect to be inviting a kid back home at that stage in their life. And they weren't trained caregivers; they hadn't chosen to spend their days helping someone eat, bathe, dress, and toilet himself. For me they would have made the sacrifice, but it wasn't something that any of us wanted.

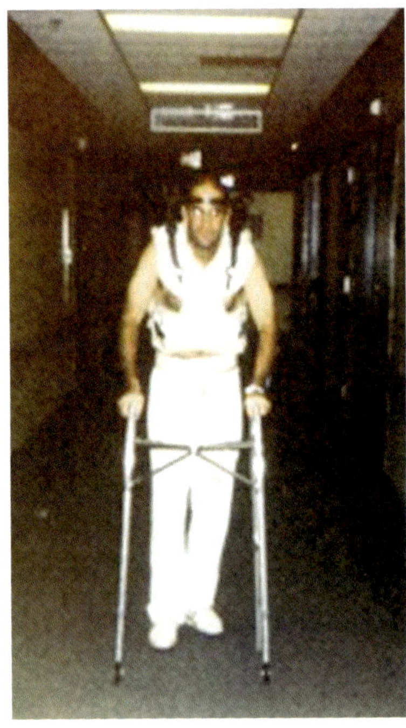

Doing laps with my grandma walker

Single cane rehab

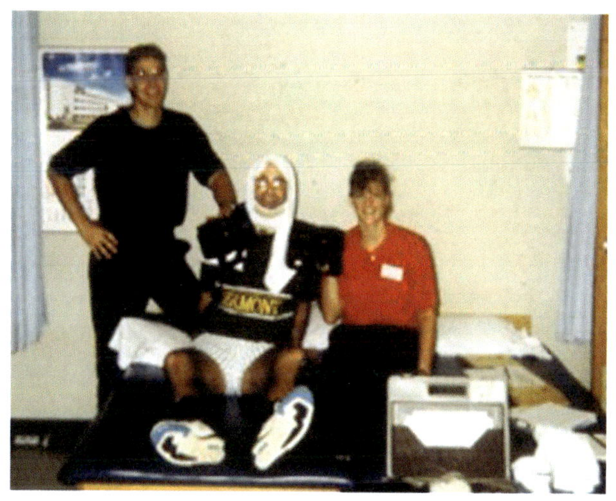

Jim & Mary, my rehab team

There was one final test I had to pass to prove that I was capable of living independently: preparing a meal. Of course, I made it easy on myself. I made one of my favorites—peanut butter (chunky) and jelly sandwiches with a side of fruit topped off with chocolate milk. Like virtually everything else since the accident, it was harder than I thought and certainly took longer than I expected. I still had a right-hand deficit to overcome, and I'd have to learn to adapt or compensate with my left hand.

Eventually, I was cleared to head back to Chicago, but my mother still accompanied me to help me settle in. Back in my bachelor pad and old environment, where everything was set up for the life I'd previously led, for the person I'd been before the accident, I began to realize just how much help I would need. I started to realize how much I had changed.

My mother encouraged me to focus on three things every day: rehabilitation, eating, and sleeping. My body had been through a catastrophic event, a near-death experience, a loss of my body functions from head to toe, a major surgery, and the beginning of physical and mental rehabilitation. The amount of rest I had been getting at the hospital wasn't enough—my mind and body were still exhausted all the time. The first night home I was in bed sleeping by seven p.m., and my mother woke me up the next day at noon. My sleeps were long and deep: sixteen to eighteen hours per day for the first few months.

But even as I grappled with the physical effects of the accident, the emotional ones besieged me. I often had terrible nightmares in which I relived the drowning episode. Waking up, I would find myself clutching the mattress to stop the bed from spinning. Many times, I would soak the sheets in fear sweat. Yes, I was back in my home, but the nightmare had come right along with me.

And still my rehabilitation continued. I had transferred my medical care to the Rehabilitation Institute of Chicago (RIC) for my outpatient treatment. It has been recognized as the number-one rehabilitation hospital in America, which certainly sounded encouraging! However, when my mom and I went in for our appointment, the staff counselor informed us,

"Your medical carrier has approved outpatient treatment for you. The sessions are once a week for fifty minutes. Your medical insurance plan has a 50 percent copay with a maximum benefit of $10,000."

As a recovering C5-C6 incomplete quadriplegic, one visit a week for fifty minutes simply wasn't going to get it done. It didn't matter if it was the best rehabilitation in the country or in the world—I needed more than that.

We decided to accept the RIC treatments while we researched other alternatives. On Monday of the following week of my return home, my mom and I went to RIC for my first session. The therapist seemed a little surprised I wasn't in a wheelchair. Later, I found out she was really wondering why I was even there; their spinal cord injury patients were generally all wheelchair bound.

When I arrived for my second session the following week, they assigned me to a different physical therapist. Upon arriving for my third session, I learned there would be yet another therapist. She introduced herself: "Hi, John, my name is Kathy Rom, R-O-M for range of motion." Right there I knew she was the right one. She would understand my desire to get back as much physical capability as possible. And I was right. She worked me hard with no apologies for the pain and strain.

Meanwhile, our research into other rehabilitation alternatives had produced two alternate options: hiring our own team, or asking for additional sessions at RIC, which we would pay for outside of my medical plan. We were puzzling over how to pay for the additional rehabilitation services, so I examined the disability policies that I owned.

The policies had a rehabilitation provision within their contract language. Both my employer-provided group LTD and my personal individual disability plans were paying me total disability benefits. This replaced a good percentage of my lost income. I had to believe they would be interested in helping me recover and get back to work and off disability faster. So I called both of the claims examiners and set up an appointment to discuss and evaluate the rehabilitation benefit options.

The group insurance carrier's claims examiner visited the next week. I met him at my office, and we spent a couple of hours discussing my medical issues: my current rehabilitation plan, daily schedule, job duties, and physician care. Two weeks later, I received a Dear John letter (in more ways than one!) from the insurance carrier.

They offered compassion for my situation but they were terminating my benefits. After reviewing my file, their staff doctor believed I could perform the substantial and material duties of my job, and that I was "choosing" to spend my time at rehabilitation. Even with a team of attorneys representing me, fighting them on this issue was a losing proposition. I learned the hard way how insufficient group long-term disability plans can be. The benefit amount wasn't enough to replace my income, wasn't enough to cover my living expenses, and the rehabilitation benefits were limited. My employer-provided group plan provided a modest level of catastrophic disability benefits, period.

Thank goodness for my private individual supplemental disability plan. The individual-carrier claims examiner came out to evaluate me as well, and a week after that, I received a letter from the insurance carrier approving the rehabilitation plan. The plan included the hiring of two physical therapists to come to my home five days a week for two hours. In addition, the plan provided for the purchase of a stationary bike, a StairMaster, and assorted weights and tools to work on my body movements and functionality. For over a year, my therapists and I worked hard on strengthening my body, building my endurance, and improving my capability. We took everything one step at a time, finding victories in each day.

It could have been so much worse. I can't imagine not being able to have had the opportunity to get back as much of my functionality as possible. Medical insurance provided the funding to put me back together, but it didn't guarantee that I would be put together like I was before the incident. It was the disability insurance and the rehabilitation benefit clause that provided the funding to improve and restore my capability to perform. Unfortunately, my story was the exception to the rule: only 31 percent of workers have long-term disability insurance to help them if they can't work.[1]

I was fortunate to have supplemented my employer-provided group long-term disability coverage with a personal individual disability plan. At the time, I never could have imagined the difference it would make. *Like most of us, I didn't know what I didn't know.*

Not all disability policies are created equal. And in my case, my individual policy made an entirely new level of recovery possible. It made the difference in the trajectory of my life, my dreams and goals, and my ability to live them out.

Without my personal disability plan, I would have been forced to accept the programs and professionals that were set in front of me, no matter how ill fitting, no matter how insufficient. I wanted my body and my life back and my personal disability plan gave me the best chance to live out my dreams and goals.

After six years of formal and informal rehabilitation, I had regained about 70 percent of my physical ability, which included walking. Today, I still have paralysis and nerve damage issues in my right hand, from my hips to the knees, and in my right foot. However, my recovery could have been considerably less complete. I came to a number of crossroads in my recovery, places where, if things had been just a little different,

1 LIFE and LIMRA "Insurance Barometer Study," 2012.

I could have wound up in a very different position. I have known such people, relegated to a living death by the seriousness of their impairment and the limits of their rehabilitation. With a lack of money and no or limited disability insurance, the daily struggle of the disability takes a toll on your body, mind, and spirit.

Accidents and illnesses can create life situations where the mind is moving so much faster than the body—where the body, in fact, cannot do the things the mind craves—that it becomes a struggle just to maintain your sanity. I know and have seen men and women lose themselves, lying in their beds all day, unable to work or function and drowning in frustration. I have heard them beg for death as their hope and dreams were gone.

My worst fears almost came true. I could have wound up living with my parents, leaning on them for everything. If I had not taken personal responsibility and purchased a private disability insurance plan, I would have found myself trapped, with no way of earning income and no assurances that I would even have enough money to live on. Statistically, one in four workers would struggle with money immediately if they were disabled and couldn't work,[2] and without my private disability plan I would have been no different.

The average life span of someone in my situation is approximately thirty years. Did I even have enough money? Do you

2 The Disability Survey conducted by Kelton Research on behalf of the LIFE Foundation, April 2012.

have enough savings to support yourself for three decades? Do you have enough to support yourself now? For three months, one year, five years?

When people think about a disabling accident or illness—if they think about it at all—they're often content to conclude that they have enough. They think there's a safety net somewhere. That someone will take care of them and it will all work itself out. But a disabling accident or illness is so much more than you can imagine. Harder, costlier, more time-consuming, and more physically, emotionally, and mentally wrenching.

It's understandable not to want to think about these things. They're scary and depressing. But facing a life of dependency, having limited choices and a complete loss of control, is even scarier. Losing huge percentages of your physical and mental capability because you can't afford appropriate medical care or rehabilitation is even more depressing. But this kind of living death can be avoided by your actions today. And don't say you didn't know—because now you do!

Oh and by the way…I never did make that million-dollar sale!

CHAPTER 2

What Is Disability, Really?

WHEN I SAY disability, what is the first thing that comes to mind? If you're like most people, you might imagine the physical objects commonly associated with illness or infirmity: hospital beds, canes, walkers, or wheelchairs. Perhaps you picture someone in a situation like mine: experiencing full or partial paralysis. I've found, in my work and in my life, that most people tend to think of disability in a few simplistic ways. They imagine disabilities as, for one, clearly visible and obvious to anyone. They imagine disabilities are the result of sudden accidents or something that happens when you get very old.

These generalizations are comforting for people because they imply that disability is something that happens either a long way off or to people unlucky enough to have a serious accident. And nothing like that could ever happen to us, right?

However, when we are speaking in terms of the legal and operative definition of disability, it's a little different. When the Social Security Administration evaluates your status as a disabled or not disabled person, it takes into account three major elements of your situation:

1. ability (or rather inability) to do work that you did prior to your disability,
2. ability (or inability) to do other types of work,
3. and expected duration of disability.

Together, these elements form the definition of disability that determines whether you receive funds from Social Security and, if so, what amount of funds. As you can tell, that definition leaves quite a bit of wiggle room for a variety of types of disability, and that definition isn't even one that everyone agrees with!

This is because disabilities are complex and widely varied. There's no one type of disability or one way to be disabled. There are thirteen thousand, six hundred ways—and counting—for the body to break down. For example, the majority of disabled people do not have a story like mine. Sudden accidents that leave someone with severely reduced capabilities actually only make up about 10 percent of all disabilities. This is surprising for many people, but it makes sense. Sudden, traumatic accidents are, fortunately, still relatively rare.

Less rare is the serious damage caused by illnesses of all types. In fact, the remaining 90 percent of all disability claims are due to various illnesses.[3] It breaks down as follows:

- 30.7 percent: diseases of the musculoskeletal system and connective tissue
- 14.2 percent: diseases of the nervous system and sense organs
- 12.1 percent: diseases of the circulatory system
- 9 percent: various cancers

These top four causes have been stable since 2010 and show no signs of budging in the future. So if you read my story and thought, *That's terrible. But that wouldn't happen to me*, maybe you're right. Statistics would seem to back up that feeling, certainly. Maybe you will never be in an accident where irreparable harm is done to your body, but can you really say that you'll never get sick? Is it really reasonable or safe to presume that you won't fall prey to an illness at any point in your life?

Additionally, assuming that disabilities are often the result of a serious accident leads people to incorrectly imagine what a

3 Council for Disability Awareness, Long-Term Disability Claims Review, 2010.

disability looks like. Even if you are very sick, you may not show the signs that others expect to see in someone disabled or someone with diminished capabilities. The weariness that comes with so many illnesses will not be obvious to those around you. Headaches, muscle pain, fatigue, motion impairments, auditory issues, mental illness—all of these are what I call invisible disabilities. And that list is really just the beginning. Anything from epilepsy to cancer can be an invisible disability.

What this means, practically, for the person with a disability, is that you are often forced to confront the misunderstandings of others. Living in a world where shorthand for disability is a wheelchair or a disfigurement, someone with an invisible disability not only has to cope with their own reduced capabilities; they are also constantly challenged to prove their disability to the world.

Personally, I have lived on both sides of these issues. During my twenty-year journey with a disability, I have gone from someone with an incredibly apparent impairment to someone who, at least outwardly, appears completely healthy. If you met me casually today, you might never know that I am a recovering ambulatory C5-C6 quadriplegic.

But the fact of the matter is, I am disabled.

Today I am no longer capable of doing the amount of work or activities I could before. I am exhausted more easily; some daily tasks are more challenging. Everything requires more energy and more recovery time. And one of the hardest aspects about getting back into the working world after my accident was helping others understand the realities of my life.

At one point, I asked for a reduced workweek because I did not have the physical ability and stamina to do the standard forty-hour week (this was already a reduction from the hard-driving schedule I was on before the accident). My boss, who was otherwise a smart and considerate person, asked if I couldn't just make calls from my bed. I didn't have a way to explain to him the trauma my body had gone through and how mentally and physically exhausting seemingly easy tasks were. I couldn't show him how my clarity of thought and ability to engage with people suffered when I was fatigued. The harder and longer I worked, the more fatigued I became. From his perspective, I looked completely normal and should have been able to operate as normal, just like before.

This, of course, can lead to a strong stigma against those with an invisible disability. Some employers may jump to a false conclusion that the disabled person is lazy or malingering rather than legitimately incapable of doing certain things. In my case, my career was especially challenging, because in many kinds of sales positions you live and die on your individual ability to hustle. If I couldn't devote hours upon hours to making contacts, developing relationships, and meeting with clients, I wasn't going to be able to earn enough money. By most measurements, my recovery and rehabilitation were extraordinary. But sometimes that isn't enough.

Many people dismiss the idea of disability insurance out of hand because they consider it a waste of money. They underestimate the chances of being disabled by an accident or illness, and they further underestimate just how much the disability will limit their ability to work. These are two great reasons why disability insurance is so critical.

Disability insurance provides you choice and control.

It goes beyond medical insurance because it provides enhanced rehabilitation treatment and the cash to choose the care you want while maintaining your lifestyle. Earlier in the chapter, I offered one definition of disability, but I have my own personal definition as well: a disability is anything that impedes your *ability* to do the amount and type of work that you did previously. I believe if you think in terms of insuring your ability and talents, rather than insuring against disability, you and many other people would be far more likely to consider personal disability insurance.

Why is it that over 80 percent of all physicians own disability insurance? They see and work with patients who have illnesses and accidents every day. And they want to protect their investment in themselves—their knowledge and skills acquired through years of schooling and training. They know very well that any reduction in their abilities will definitely result in a loss of income.

Are your talents, skills, and abilities worth protecting? Yes, they are!

CHAPTER 3

Abilities Create Capital

MAYBE DISABILITY INSURANCE should be called ability insurance. Ability insurance comes down to one major idea: protecting the capabilities that earn your income so you can enjoy the lifestyle you have created, live out your dreams and goals, secure your existing assets, and protect the financial security of you and your loved ones.

For the most part, we are historically bad at planning for our futures, period. Believe it or not, some people argue that they don't need disability insurance because that's what their retirement funds are for. Unfortunately, if you're like the vast majority of people, you probably haven't saved enough to cover even an uneventful retirement.

The unfortunate truth is that many, many people don't do enough to protect the things that are the most important or valuable to them. Some people spend more time (and money) planning and insuring their least valuable assets—lower priority material assets—against even the smallest risks.

What would you do to be certain that, if you became sick or hurt, you would still be able to remain in your home? What would you do to be certain that you wouldn't have to prematurely empty your checking account, savings account, retirement plan, or your child's education fund? One of the most challenging issues about becoming sick or hurt is simply not being able to do things that once came easily and automatically to you. Wouldn't it be better and easier to have a plan in place that enabled you to take *control* and have *choice* within your life?

Where to begin? First of all, you have to seriously evaluate how much you are worth. And when I say that, I am not talking about the house, the car, and the savings. I am talking about your value as human capital. What is your human capital?

Calculate yours here:
http://www.drgdi.com/ppphlc

It is your unique set of skills and knowledge that allows you to perform work that produces an economic value. (*Cash!*)

You acquire human capital in a number of ways: on-the-job experience, education, training, even natural talent. Most of us spend our entire working lives accruing human capital and, like anything else of value, we invest in it in the form of education, on- and off-the-job training, health and wellness care, as well as diet and exercise.

To help conceptualize this idea, I've developed an exercise that I'd like to do with you. It's called Your Name Inc. and it's just what it sounds like. Imagine, for a moment, that you are a business, and like any business, you have assets and liabilities that make up your balance sheet. It helps to actually create a real balance sheet with pen and paper and jot down this information. To further assist you, I've created one for you.

On one side of the sheet, list all of your assets. For our purposes here, I mean all of your existing funds, such as investments, checking/savings, and retirement accounts. Also include all your property, like the car(s), house(s), and furniture, etc.

On the other side of the page, list all your liabilities, including any student loans, credit card balances, mortgages, or other debts that you may have. Now subtract your liabilities from your assets to determine the net worth of Your Name Inc. (See Appendix A.)

Balance Sheet of Your Name Inc.

ASSETS	LIABILITIES
Bank accounts	Debts
Toys/Valuables	Mortgage
House	Credit cards
Stocks and bonds	Student loans
Cars	
Pension	
Total: $________	**Total:** $________
+ **HUMAN CAPITAL** $________	
Net Worth Grand Total $ ________	

Note: HUMAN CAPITAL is converted to financial capital as you age.

Assets + HUMAN CAPITAL – Debts and Liabilities = Net Worth

But that number is not the whole story. With the concept of human capital, we measure what you have as well as your future potential. That potential is made up of your future possible earnings. For example, if you earn $100,000 a year and you intend to work for twenty more years, you would add a human capital number of $2,000,000 to your asset side. ($100,000 x 20 = $2,000,000.) Interested? Maybe your potential is even more. Go ahead and add in raises and bonus income to the human capital number.

Now ask yourself: Is that number worth protecting? Think about what that number represents: hope. You are hoping you will have twenty healthy and productive years ahead of you in which your talent and abilities earn the income. You hope that the $2,000,000 will be there for you and those you love. You are counting on your income to continue to provide your lifestyle and help you achieve your dreams and goals.

When it comes to protection, I prefer to push the big risks off on the insurance companies and self-insure against the smaller risks. To this end, my automobile and home owner deductibles are higher than average. Why pay more for a $200 deductible when you can afford a $1,000 one and a bad event is less likely? I'd rather pay less for the higher deductible and use the savings to fully insure the big risks.

Our biggest risk is the loss of our talents and capabilities—our ability to create human capital. I fully insure my human capital. I choose to do more than just hope that nothing bad happens to me. Protect your human capital—insure against the biggest of risks! Obtaining a personal disability insurance plan is the best way to avoid compounding a physical disaster with a financial one.

To give you a real-life example of how this kind of assessment can change your future planning, I'll share with you the story of Dr. Tom. I met with Dr. Tom and his accountant, Jim, in 2012. He wasn't an entirely new client, but I hadn't walked him through the idea of human capital yet. After a few minutes of discussion, I took out a blank sheet of paper and wrote, "Dr. Tom Inc.," at the top center. To the left and right, I wrote "assets" and "liabilities." I handed the paper to Dr. Tom and his accountant and asked them to list out the assets and liabilities for Dr. Tom Inc.

After Dr. Tom completed the exercise, I wrote "net worth" on the bottom right side of the paper and asked Jim to calculate the net worth of Dr. Tom Inc. He proceeded to write in the number and then handed the paper back to me. With a puzzled look, I asked, "What are we missing here?" Dr. Tom wasn't sure, so I wrote "human capital" on the asset side, with a question mark, and handed the paper back to him.

Of course, he didn't understand yet what human capital meant. I explained the concept to him and we discussed the value of his income as an asset and its future value. Of course, as a physician, Dr. Tom had a very high earning potential, and his human capital number put Dr. Tom Inc. well into the black.

Suddenly, it was as though the proverbial lightbulb had gone on in his head. We multiplied Tom's current income by the number of years he wanted to work; even though we assumed no salary increases, the number still surprised him. He'd never thought of his career in those terms, and seeing the number written out like that underscored how valuable his time, talent, and abilities really were.

I asked Dr. Tom, "Would you be interested in protecting your hope? May I show you how to preserve your future human capital value?"

It wasn't as though Dr. Tom didn't know how much he made per year; he just had taken it for granted that he would continue earning the money, uninterrupted. He assumed the money would always be there, without ever really thinking about how much money it was, and how much he would have to cover if that income stream suddenly disappeared.

Most of us live our lives one day at a time. We work hard to provide for ourselves and our families, pay our bills, fund our lifestyles, and purchase the things that bring us joy. It's easy to forget that our future is never guaranteed. If you want to continue living your life as you are, or are even aiming higher, you need to plan for that.

Dan Sullivan, CEO of The Strategic Coach, taught me to

ask myself and my clients the following future-based question. It's a question I'd like you to consider answering.

"If we were meeting here, three years from today, and you were looking back over those three years—back to today—what has to have happened over those three years, both personally and professionally, for you to feel happy with your progress?"

Overwhelmingly, people want to improve. Very few clients tell me they want everything to just stay the same. You want to advance in your career, you want to develop your skills, you want to have a more secure nest egg—the list goes on. All of those things are possible—even likely—for most people. However, there is always the danger of the unknown when we are thinking about our future. You cannot mistake wanting for planning. And you cannot mistake assuming for knowing.

It's just not enough to hope; you need to safeguard that hope from obstacles that you may not see coming. Because, as I learned firsthand, hope is so much more fragile than we realize.

CHAPTER 4

Aren't I Covered Already?

ON A FLIGHT back home, I started chatting with Jim, the gentleman next to me. After the usual introductory comments and questions, I asked how he liked working for a *Fortune* 1,000 company. He mentioned that he enjoyed the work and travel. He had been working there for about eight years and was being promoted about every other year. Then I asked what he would do if he wasn't able to work, if he had an accident or illness that prevented his ability to work. He paused a bit and then looked at me and said, "I hope my employer will take care of me."

In the same way that people don't like to think about having a disabling accident or illness, they also like to assume that they are already covered—and that their coverage is the type and amount they need. Better yet, many believe their medical insurance alone is good enough. That should take care of any medical problem. Right?

Imagine that you obtain a great job in your industry. It's everything you could want from an employer and when you come on board, you are enrolled in the company's group medical insurance plan. Great news!

The plan itself is a long, dense document full of high-level medical and economic terms. It's easy for you to brush the plan aside. You're busy with actual work, after all, and the language of the plan wasn't written for you; it was written for doctors or maybe lawyers. It's free (mostly) health care, your doctor(s) are in the network, and that's all you really need to know. You toss the employer manual and benefits paperwork into your desk drawer.

But then, several years later, your life changes. Perhaps you get into a serious car accident or, more likely, you develop an illness that drastically reduces your ability to do your work. Your life has been transformed and every day brings a new set of problems you never thought you'd have to deal with. At least you have your employer's group medical insurance. The medical insurance helps you obtain the treatments you need, but the recovery will be long and maybe there is a permanent condition you will have to learn to live with the rest of your life. The hospital, the doctors, the nurses, and even the ambulance driver all get paid through the medical insurance plan. *What about you?*

Your employer continues to pay you, but it's only your sick time, personal days, vacation, and that's it. How long did that last? Did you sign up for the disability plan? *I think they had some sort of short-term and long-term disability plan, but it's been so long since I looked at the benefits package...*

Your next call is to the HR benefits director to find out what you have—you're hoping that you checked all the right boxes, including the disability benefits box. You will now depend on it to provide the cash while you are out of work. You learn that you have disability coverage and even better, the employer has been paying for the disability benefit plan. At first, it seems like a huge relief.

However, you quickly become acquainted with all the details of your plan, including a number of unpleasant surprises. First, you can't get the maximum income replacement you need by using only this plan. In terms of income coverage, your group long-term disability plan only provides up to 60 percent of your prior income. If your annual income is $100,000, 60 percent of that is $60,000. Is that enough?

You're still adjusting to that fact when you learn the benefit is treated like taxable income. That's because your employer pays for this employee benefit. So the 60 percent—$60,000—will be further reduced by taxes. You will now have to live and survive on 50 percent of your income—maybe less. Can you afford that kind of pay cut?

Now you're starting to get worried.

Like most people, you haven't saved nearly enough to

cover this kind of eventuality. Even among those who have established a nest egg, that's intended to get them through retirement, not through a prolonged disability in the middle of their income-earning years. You could be disabled for five, ten, twenty—maybe even more than thirty years.

At this point, you are doing everything you can to speed up your recovery and get some of your capability back. But again you face a roadblock here. Your employer's medical insurance plan covered the majority of your medical expenses, such as the surgeries, medicine, doctors, and any hospital stays. The goal of the medical insurance is to put you back together as best they can; there is no guarantee you will be back together the way you were before the accident or illness. You find it's much, much harder to qualify for funds to obtain rehabilitation services. Medical insurance benefits only go so far. And they certainly don't pay your salary.

The medical insurance plan does not guarantee doctors will be able to put the patient back together just the way they were before. That's because, in many cases, it's simply not possible. Medical professionals try their best, but every illness and accident is different and every person responds differently. So there is no telling or predicting what the outcome may be, how long it will take or how close to your old self you will return.

Another surprise happens when you speak with the group long-term disability claims examiner. Your status as disabled is at the mercy of the physicians who are associated with the group disability insurance company. Professionals you didn't choose, who most likely don't treat you on a daily basis, will now decide whether or not you are able to work. If they do assess that you are capable of working, of performing the substantial and material duties of your job, your benefits may stop.

This may seem like an extreme example, but it happened to me. About twelve months after my accident, I decided to start coming into the office a couple of times a week. It only amounted to maybe an hour each time. I would open mail, speak with a few clients and coworkers and let them know my status. It was the very beginning of the back-to-work process. I missed seeing and working with my team and customers. I wanted them to know I was going to be back at some point.

And maybe I was telling *myself* that I was going to be back. My psychiatrist at the time said this was good for my mental healing. It helped me envision a positive future self. I wasn't doing anything that could meaningfully be called work, but it was important, psychologically, for me to go in and be productive to the degree that I was able.

However, as soon as the group long-term disability insurance carrier's claims examiner learned that I was working, they sent an examiner out to do an assessment. A week after meeting with the examiner, I received a Dear John letter.

The letter explained that my benefits would be terminating.

They (their staff physicians) ruled that I was capable of performing the "substantial and material duties" of my job. If I wasn't working, it was because I was "choosing" to continue rehabilitation. This was coming from doctors who didn't treat me, who only knew about me and my recovery from an interview. I'd come in, sort some mail, and speak with a few clients. But that was enough to shut down my benefits through the group long-term disability insurance carrier.

I was so fortunate; I had a private individual disability insurance plan. My doctor—the physician who had actually worked with me and was familiar with my case—understood immediately that I was not ready to return to part-time let alone full-time work. I can't imagine how my rehabilitation (and my life) would have been set back had I needed to try and return to a nine-to-five job at that point. Quite frankly, at that time, I was unable to function nine to five at work, at home, or anywhere else.

Unfortunately, this is the reality for many, many people in the United States. We are comforted by the idea of the medical and disability insurance plans through our employers. We don't really try to learn what that means. Group insurance plans are great benefits, no question, however, they absolutely have limitations. Group long-term disability plans provide great catastrophic benefits. These types of plans are designed to offer a modest benefit to the largest number of people at the lowest possible cost. That's the bottom line. They are not designed to offer the best care, the highest quality, or highest income replacement benefit to people.

Group long-term disability insurance is significantly less expensive than individual disability insurance. That's because group long-term disability plans provide coverage for a large amount of people (the more people insured, the more the cost can be amortized among them). And the coverage terms are not comprehensive—they are catastrophic.

Individual disability insurance is more expensive. However, it's simply a case of getting what you pay for. Individual disability insurance covers more types of accidents and illnesses that cause a disability. Typically it covers them for longer period of time, and it provides more benefits and services.

Individual disability plans put the choice and control in your hands and the hands of your treating physicians. If you're suffering from an accident or an illness, chances are there are already a great many things in your life you can't control. Why not grab hold of the reins to the things you *can*?

Group LTD and individual disability plans have their own merits and, in the end, it may not be about choosing one or the other. How about having both types of coverage? Individual disability insurance is a great supplement to an employer-provided group long-term disability plan. And here are three reasons why:

1. Group LTD covers the catastrophic events while the individual LTD provides both catastrophic and comprehensive coverage. The two types of coverage can work together to provide everything that you need, to include benefits for total and partial disability, recovery benefits, back-to-work benefits, rehabilitation services, and even training and equipment if needed.

2. By having both types of plans, you maximize the amount of income that is replaced and the benefit amount payable to you. The combination of both allows for greater replacement of your income. Instead of 60 percent replacement, you may have up to 80 percent replacement of your income.

3. When you own an individual policy, the policy goes wherever you go. You may voluntarily or involuntarily change jobs. Your employer may reduce or stop offering a group long-term disability plan. Any number of events could cause an interruption to your policy and having one that is bound to you—not an employer—circumvents this problem and keeps you in control.

Now, the big issue on everyone's mind right now is the Patient Protection and Affordable Care Act (or Obamacare) and what that will mean in terms of existing medical insurance plans. It's too early to tell exactly what is going to happen, but one thing is certain: many, many more people are going to have access to medical services. That's a good thing! The even better news comes from a medical insurance standpoint: the ACA (Obamacare) provides the ability to have access to portable medical insurance regardless of your medical circumstances or employment.

However, the ACA does present some real issues in terms of how we will accommodate this new influx of patients who need care. Even before the ACA went into effect, we were facing a shortage of physicians in this country. It's so severe, in fact, the Association of American Medical Colleges estimates the shortage at around ninety thousand in the next decade. Several state and federal programs have been put in place to encourage more young people to attend medical school. However, those young people still need time to complete their schooling and do their residencies before they can really get out in the field. We are easily talking about four to eight years before that influx of new physicians starts practicing in our hospitals and clinics. Undeniably, the shortage of physicians will have an effect on the type and quality of care that the consumer can expect.

Additionally, we have seen a major shift in the past decade in how our society and employers think about health care. Instead of the employer-sponsored and paid for comprehensive health care that was a fixture of previous generations, the onus is increasingly put upon the individual—the employee—to take personal responsibility for their financial and health care future.

You can no longer rely on the government or your employer to provide you with the best of the best insurance for the rest of your life—or even fund your retirement with a pension. The Social Security Administration estimates that the average monthly disability payment from Social Security is a paltry $1,110[4] per month. The days of an external safety net are disappearing. We live in a world today where, if you want something done right, you have to do it yourself—personal responsibility!

If you want the maximum disability income benefit (up to 70 to 80 percent of your income, instead of 50 to 60 percent), if you want the best possible health recovery care, if you want the most intensive rehabilitation plan, if you want the longest benefit payment time periods, the highest benefit caps, if you really want the best chance at the best possible recovery and financial stability, then you need to buy your own disability insurance plan, *period.* Make the choice to take control of your

4 Social Security Administration.

health and your lifestyle to insure you have the best opportunity to live a life that is truly life.

To further prove the point, as the ACA (Obamacare) becomes fully implemented, you and most other consumers will have higher deductibles, face higher copayment amounts, higher coinsurance levels, and tighter limits on coverage for out-of-network care. Even the accepted network of physicians will become smaller and the covered medical treatments terms more restrictive.

According to a McKinsey & Co. analysis, nearly 50 percent of all Obamacare plans are tightly managed HMOs. In states like California, Missouri, and New Hampshire, many networks are 40 or 45 percent the size of those offered for normal commercial coverage. Many patients will have to deal with longer waiting periods or geographically inconvenient providers. Many people may be forced to sacrifice additional medical options to obtain a lower initial cost/premium. Individuals and families who choose midlevel plans will have an annual plan deductible of about $2,900 for an individual and $6,100 for a family. The average annual out-of-pocket spending maximum will be about $5,700 for an individual and $11,500 for a family.

Many insurance companies recognized the high deductible problem and have already prepared for the year of the gap fillers by announcing new worksite supplemental medical product programs. These programs will provide benefits to fill the gaps of the high deductible plans. The additional cost is used to provide supplemental benefits, such as ER and urgent care visits and outpatient X-rays, among other services. The insurance companies know there is a huge financial gap problem that is being put on individuals and families choosing midlevel plans.

However, research is showing that when people have to make a choice with their money for their health, they prioritize comprehensive care, quality, choice, and control. The *Wall Street Journal* said last year, "Some 82.5 percent of eHealth customers in 2012 purchased preferred provider organization plans (PPOs) that are structured so patients can visit virtually any physician."[5]

Adding an individual disability plan to your overall health program will provide you the ultimate in comprehensive health care with empowerment of choice, control, and cash. Medical insurance plans only go so far, and they don't pay you. When you become too sick or hurt to work, individual disability insurance is the ultimate gap filler to enhance your medical insurance into a more comprehensive health plan—and it pays you.

Don't let the disruption of the ACA convince you that all is okay with your medical insurance and overall health care plans.

5 http://online.wsj.com/news/articles/SB10001424052702303460004579192081764514664?mod=trending_now_1.

Disruption is everywhere and is affecting all of us. Some of the disruption is positive and some negative. And the disruption is in so many areas of our lives, from important areas like health care, retirement planning, and education to the mundane yet necessary (phones, shopping, and television). How do you focus and decide? How do you prioritize where to spend your time and money?

CHAPTER 5

Defining Your Purpose —The Whole-Person Health Plan

***DILBERT* IS ONE** of my favorite comic strips. It is written by Scott Adams, who wrote an article that I believe astutely lays out the equation for a happy life.[6] He renders it simply:

Happiness = Freedom + Health

In my experience, however, I would add an additional component, so my equation would look like:

Happiness = Freedom + Health + Purpose^2

Purpose is a critical element (that's why it's squared!). Purpose gets each and every one of us out of bed in the morning. It pushes us to engage with the world, to feel and experience, to make a difference in the lives of others, to grow ourselves and expand our freedom, health, and, ultimately, our

6 http://www.washingtonpost.com/business/read-this-if-you-want-to-be-happy-in-2014/2014/01/02/d96370f0-7192-11e3-9389-09ef9944065e_story.html.

happiness. Weighting purpose more heavily actually amplifies all the other elements.

However, if even one of these elements is eliminated, the equation doesn't work anymore. When you are disabled, it disrupts every single one of these elements. Your life equation no longer makes sense. Your happiness is imperiled. Owning an individual disability plan gave me the freedom to design and seek out my own medical and rehabilitative care, which, in turn, allowed me to recover more fully. Just as important, it allowed me to use my restored talents and capabilities to chase down my purpose and live out my dreams and goals. My happiness was directly connected to the choice and security my disability insurance benefits offered me.

For me, learning and putting into practice the wisdom of successful people has been instrumental for my success in life. One of them is Stephen Covey. He famously wrote *The Seven Habits of Highly Effective People*, which has been an important part of my life for the last fifteen years. Two of his concepts in particular have really changed the way I operate in my day-to-day life: beginning with the end in mind, and the four-box quadrant. Starting with the end in mind has helped me clarify my dreams and goals before I begin striving toward them. What do you want your life to look like? Can you visualize it in detail?

The four-box quadrant helped me prioritize my actions and behaviors. It works like this:

Urgent and Important	Important and Not Urgent
Urgent and Not Important	Not Urgent and Not Important

The idea is that you sort all of your activities into the following four categories. This allows you some critical perspective on what is really most important and improves your time management immensely. Here's an example of the types of activities that go into each category:

Urgent and Important Last-minute changes to schedule, phone calls, reactionary behaviors, FedEx packages, day-to-day work that is on deadline.	**Important and Not Urgent** Working out, thinking strategically, planning, learning, reading, going to the dentist, creative work, recreation and family time.
Urgent and Not Important Low-value work and play, required reports, administrative and busy work.	**Not Urgent and Not Important** Pointless Web surfing, time wasting, watching television, gossiping.

Now, how does this fit into health care and disability coverage? Well, this sort of diagram is useful in helping people prioritize life's activities. Many times you don't have a good sense of how much of your valuable—and limited—time you spend on the things that are not important until you see it written down. Furthermore, many of us have a tendency to dismiss whatever is not urgent, no matter how important it may be.

Obtaining disability insurance falls into the latter category. For most of us, disability insurance is important but not urgent (unless you're going bungee jumping later today). There is a high probability that you will get through today without an accident or illness. In fact, you probably won't become disabled this week or this month. But this year? Next year? The next five years? We have a way of ignoring nonurgent tasks until they become emergencies.

Instead, why not plan to protect your income, your health, and quality of your life instead of just reacting to a catastrophe? You would never jump out of an airplane with a poorly packed parachute, after all. But if you have started your working life without making this type of plan, that's exactly what you are doing. Today, you have the talents and abilities to earn an income—you have jumped out of the plane and you are on your way down. How are you going to land?

So, what is the future health of *you*? This goes beyond medical care—the elements of your future health take into account comprehensive care, quality, choice, and control over medical care to include physical, mental, and even lifestyle health. Your future health is a whole-person approach to health care, not just medical care.

The choices you make regarding the food you eat, the activity you participate in and even the content you feed your mind all contribute to your whole-person health.

In a keynote presentation at an American Academy of Pediatrics conference, Dr. Atul Gawande shared a concept from a friend of his on the future success of patient health care. He believes we are in the midst of the "century of the system"—a coordinated web of different elements of health care that will determine the best outcome for the patient.

With this concept, systems could be applied to the coordination of a surgery with a person's financial foundation. Imagine having your whole-person health care interconnected and so perfectly balanced that you can live to your highest potential in terms of health, wellness, and nutrition. Meanwhile, you still have the security of knowing that in your time of medical need, the care you receive will provide the best outcomes for your physical and mental being while also providing income replacement, rehabilitation, and return-to-work services. Throughout this time of difficulty, your financial foundation remains intact and your cash flow—your income—continues to allow you to fulfill your financial commitments and provide daily necessities for yourself. Think now about the products and services you may need to support that kind of whole-person health. A pictorial representation of a whole-person health system might look like the graphic below.

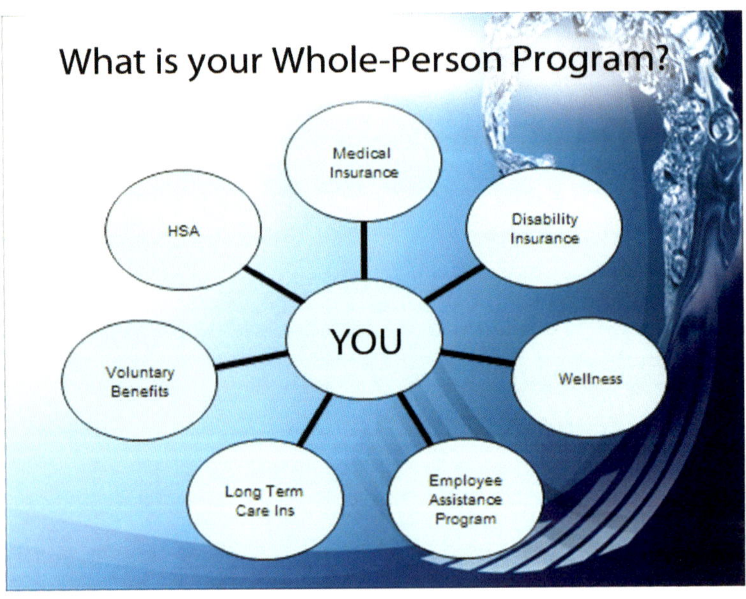

Now, how does that boilerplate medical insurance plan stack up in comparison? I'm guessing not very well!

CHAPTER 6

The Domino Effect — Protecting Your Relationships

"Never let your family, significant others, or those close to you pay a price for your lack of self-discipline or responsibility."
—Harry Hoopis

THERE IS SOMETHING special about starting a family. It changes your entire perspective. Suddenly, the choices you made before and the things you value start to shift. For the first time, you can see, up close and personal, the responsibility you have for others and how your life, your choices, and your behavior affect theirs. Nothing is just about you anymore and now all the decisions you make unavoidably include another person—maybe several other people.

At the time of my accident, I barely knew what being a quadriplegic would mean for me, let alone what it would mean for the people I loved.

I actually married while I was still recovering and rehabilitating my mind, body, and spirit. My treating psychiatrist tried to convince me not to do it, to persuade me that getting married at this time was just not a good decision. I thought my psychiatrist was just another naysayer, trying to tell me what else I couldn't do. It seemed like I had heard "you can't" every hour of every day since the accident. My neurosurgeon didn't think I would walk again—I proved *him* wrong and I would prove my psychiatrist wrong as well.

And I did. It's easy to get married, after all—if it wasn't, a lot of people in Las Vegas would need to rethink their business model. What's hard is staying married—it was especially hard for a recovering C5-C6 quadriplegic who was always thinking about himself and his daily struggle. I was always tired. It took everything I had just to deal with myself and my recovery; I had very little left, emotionally, physically, and mentally, for another person. I didn't have the energy to live a normal life. Relationships are a two-way street and at this time in my life, it was all about me. It couldn't be any other way if I was going to maximize my potential recovery physically and mentally.

For my wife, the person I was after my accident and during rehabilitation was materially different from the man she thought she'd married. Neither of us ever really talked about my disability. From the outside looking in, you might not have even known I was disabled at that point. On the inside of my body and mind, however, everything was different.

My wife experienced firsthand my constant fatigue that regularly forced me to reject her; she witnessed my lack of engagement, the burden of my health condition, and my self-focused daily schedule. This is not the way anyone wants to live and no one plans for this—we certainly didn't ever imagine that this would be our future together.

I'm sure she asked herself every day, "How long is this recovery going to take? When will he be back to normal? One year, two, three, five…forever? Is he ever going to be active again?"

Relationships are about serving each other, about putting your own needs aside for the good of your partner and your relationship. At the time, being newly disabled and focusing on rehabilitation, I wasn't serving my bride very well, if at all. It was all about me, my health, and my recovery to get back to normal—back to work, back to the John Nichols prior to the accident. I didn't have anything inside me for anyone else, not even the love of my life. Hard as I tried, I was still a burden to those closest to me and it had a disastrous effect on all of us. Quite frankly, *I* wouldn't have wanted to be married to me.

In retrospect, the psychiatrist was right, though I hate to admit it. Marriage is hard enough for healthy, active, and normal people. I had set myself up for failure right out of the gate by jumping the gun and pushing too hard, too fast. Instead of waiting until I was whole and ready to really share in building a marriage, I embroiled someone in my own recovery, which inevitably placed her in the unwanted role of caregiver.

This brings to the forefront another issue that many young and middle-aged people have: you are between natural caregivers. While no one wants to move back in with their mother and father for round-the-clock care, it is at least possible for a couple of people in their fifties to care for a disabled person. As you age, your parents age, and they become less and less of a resource and safety net for you. Would you really ask your seventy-five- or eighty-year-old parent to care for you, day in and day out? Instead of one disabled person, you might quickly wind up with two or three!

Similarly, people in older age ranges often have grown children they can lean on. This is hardly the most desirable solution to the problem, but it is a theoretical solution. This isn't an option for people in their mid-thirties to early forties, who may have children still in grade school. In fact, it's much the reverse: your children still need you to provide for them, even if you're disabled.

This brings us to an even greater concern—your responsibilities. They don't just go away when you become injured or sick. In your thirties and forties, it is common to start taking on greater and greater responsibilities. You are getting married, maybe having children, attempting to set down roots, maybe even purchasing a house. How will you make sure that you can always take care of the people who depend on you?

Hopefully, if you have children, you have life insurance. Now, it only makes sense to buy disability insurance at the same time. Unfortunately, many people have not been educated on how disability insurance can benefit them. Instead, they see it as just another bill. For people who are building their families and establishing a lifestyle, another bill is the last thing that they need. Disability insurance seems unknown and even intangible, especially as people don't think anything could ever happen to them. It's easier to rationalize disability insurance as an unnecessary expense that only serves to soothe your anxieties.

The reality is far different. If you were to pass away unexpectedly and you had life insurance, that money would go directly to your family. Even though they would no longer have your income stream to support them, they would have some degree of financial security (and a positive legacy provided by you). If you are disabled, not only is your family losing your income, but your care and rehabilitation are actively putting a financial strain on your family as a whole. You become a burden physically, emotionally, and financially. Financially, you could literally be better off dead if you don't have a comprehensive personal disability insurance plan.

Emotionally, it was a difficult time when my wife and I decided to divorce. Financially, however, my disability insurance meant that I didn't have to shoulder the additional worries of how to navigate a divorce on top of my rehabilitation and disability. Because of my disability insurance plans, our financial foundation and affairs were in great shape. We were able to part ways without any lasting negative financial implications such as bad credit scores, heavy debt, missed payments, or bankruptcy. We didn't have to unnecessarily sell off our possessions or cash in mutual funds and stock portfolios. Proactive planning and good choices and decisions lead to better and happier outcomes!

Something many people fail to understand about disability is the mental and emotional component. Physically, as we age we are less and less capable of bouncing back from even minor accidents and illnesses, let alone the kind of catastrophic event that I went through. On the flip side, the mental toughness that allows us to adapt to new situations and resist depression actually grows as we age. Experiencing a loss of capability can be even more disastrous for a younger person than someone suffering a disability later in life.

It's true that people in older age brackets have more trouble recovering physically, but that doesn't mean we should discount the role that positive mental energy plays in the process. When I was in recovery, I needed everything I had, mentally and emotionally, just to keep striving forward. If I had been distraught with worry over money or not being able to settle the divorce properly, I would have severely set myself back.

Of course, what I also learned from this experience was our responsibility to another person doesn't necessarily go away with the end of the relationship. This is even truer if you have children. The income protection component of disability insurance may provide the money for the alimony and child care payments. It may be the difference for your children—who had nothing to do with your disability—between living out their potential or suffering along with you for years on end.

Disability insurance is a choice that you make; however, the outcome of your decision is simply so much bigger than you are. When evaluating whether or not to obtain this kind of coverage, think about those who do not have a voice in the matter yet who will benefit or suffer all the same.

When you eschew disability insurance, you are putting your relationships at risk. If, at some point, you do become disabled and you lack income protection, you have now limited the trajectory of your entire family. What schools they attend, where they live, how they live, whether they'll be able to attend college: these and many more are life issues that can change in the blink of an eye. Many parents with kids are thinking constantly about their children's futures. They're socking away money in retirement funds or college saving plans and trying to save some of their income toward the future.

But an accident or illness can wipe out those savings in just a few short months or years. Furthermore, the accident or illness hampers—or stops entirely—your ability to save while you're unable to work and earn an income. When I had my accident, I lost six years of retirement funding. You cannot make up for lost time, especially when it comes to savings that grow and build on the previous assets. Disability insurance protects your ability to earn an income, but it is even more than that: it is a savings protection plan, and a lifestyle and time protector. It is a protection plan that encompasses relationships in your life—the people you love and those you strive to provide for.

Life is about more than you, hence the domino effect. You can't choose whether or not that first domino will fall, but you can choose whether the impact will be negative or positive. The choice is yours.

CHAPTER 7

A Millennial Mind-set — Live Your Cause

IF THERE IS anything that the accumulated articles, books, studies, and op-eds about millennials have taught us, it's that they are not playing by the old rules. Studies show that millennials have very different priorities when it comes to what they want out of work and out of their lives. They want to believe in a cause and make a tangible difference. Money is important, but impact is just as important—maybe more.

Millennials grew up in a time of economic uncertainty, where the old models of joining a company right out of school and staying there until retirement just don't hold up anymore. Instead, millennials are known for frequent job—even career—changes, regarding their work as fundamentally temporary. Family, friends, and balance of life are highly valued.

For this generation, employer group insurance plans are especially ill fitting. What happens to your group insurance plans when you decide to move on to another company? What if you are fired? What if you decide to break away and go freelance or even start your own business? Millennials are more entrepreneurial than any other generation in the workforce now.

How would it affect your business if you suffered an illness or accident that put you out of work with no paycheck for any length of time? How would it affect your family and friends?

Individual disability insurance plans have two great features that make them ideal for this lifestyle: they are portable, and they provide 24-7 coverage. You own your policy and you can take it wherever you go. It is not beholden to any particular employer, any particular doctor, or even any particular treatment. When I decided to start my rehabilitation after the accident, I looked into the rehabilitation provision on my medical insurance plan. If you'll recall, the plan had a maximum benefit payment cap of $10,000 with a 50-percent copay, and I qualified for one fifty-minute outpatient session a week. This is crazy. There was absolutely no way that level of medical care was going to be enough for a recovering C5-C6 quadriplegic.

My individual disability insurance benefits provided me some much-needed choice and control. Instead of mandating a certain amount and duration of physical therapy, my disability insurance plan paid me cash that I could use at my own discretion. I hired an occupational and a physical therapist. They came to my house for two hours a day, five days a week, for over a year. That was the level of care I needed to give myself the best chance at maximizing my recovery and I never would have received it without my individual disability insurance benefits.

I really can't stress enough the importance of intensive, long-term rehabilitative care. It is the difference between surviving and living. I had a neighbor with an injury similar to mine. Unlike me, however, he was never able to obtain the rehabilitation he needed. He spent twenty years in bed with only his family to care for him and meet all of his daily needs. In a moment of honesty, he admitted to me that he prayed the same prayer every day: that he wouldn't wake up the next morning.

My neighbor was tired. He was tired of being cared for by his loved ones. He grew tired of seeing their exhaustion and pain. He was tired of suffering, lying in bed day in and day out. Tired of not being able to do the work that he loved and live out his life's dreams and goals. He was tired of merely surviving.

If you do not protect your ability to do the things that you love, what do you have left?

Too often, younger people fall into a pattern of thinking of themselves and their bodies as invincible. We expect our cars will wear out. We expect our homes might be flooded or catch fire. We understand objects that are important to us need to be protected but, for some reason, that understanding rarely extends to our bodies. Unfortunately, this type of thinking is dead wrong: one in four of today's twenty-year-olds will become disabled before they retire.[7]

More and more in the current economic climate, people are going into the workforce with the understanding that they will need to keep working longer than their parents or grandparents.

7 Social Security Administration, Basic Facts, Feb. 7, 2013.

Many Americans are planning to work into their late sixties or early seventies. Can you really say that, over the course of forty or fifty years, your body is never going to suffer some sort of accident, some sort of illness? Will you be fit and spry and as capable of work at forty-five as you are at twenty-eight?

Individual disability insurance can seem like an unnecessary expense, however, when you consider what you are getting for your money…it is worth it. Doesn't it make sense to invest a little bit of your current income to protect your capability—the skills and talents that allow you to earn an income and accomplish your goals and dreams?

Twenty-one percent of young adults say they don't have disability insurance because their jobs aren't physical.[8] Nevertheless, our skills and talents are about more than just our material bodies. Even if you have a white-collar job with no physical requirement, how will you protect against the loss of energy and mental acuity that so often comes with from an accident or illness? And if your human capital isn't valuable enough, what about your dignity and independence?

Millennials are already prepared to shoulder most of the burdens of their financial future. Programs like Social Security have been teetering on the brink of bankruptcy since most of these people were in grade school. The younger generation

8 LearnVest/Guardian White, "Life and Disability Insurance: What 20- and 30-somethings Think," 2013..

understands that the responsibility for retirement savings will fall mainly on their shoulders, absent those comprehensive government social programs and the traditional employer pension system.

Quite frankly, even if the government and employer programs provide some level of retirement income, it will be at a level well below what you are used to living on. Most millennials would consider it practical and reasonable to have some sort of retirement savings. Why not also protect the stream of income that allows you to have that savings in the first place?

It's undeniably true that young people carry more debt than older generations.[9] It's understandable to feel cash strapped, but the simple facts are there is always a way to get what you really need and there is always an excuse not to do something. After all, 57 percent of young adults have seen the value of life insurance, versus the paltry 35 percent who have disability insurance.[10] Disability insurance is not nice to have—it's a must-have!

Disability insurance offers you a steady and consistent stream of income if you are unable to work due to a sickness or accident. More than any one thing, disability insurance

---

9 http://finance.yahoo.com/news/why-generation-x-had-the-worst-personal-finance-year-ever-214519220.html?goback=%2Egde_3823648_member_5818376075675205635#%21.

10 LearnVest/Guardian White, "Life and Disability Insurance: What 20- and 30-somethings Think," 2013.

protects your ability to have and maintain your lifestyle, your relationships, your material possessions, and your financial well-being as well as the more intangible and just as important things: self-reliance, choice, control, recovery, and your dreams for the future.

CHAPTER 8

Don't Take My Word for It

ANY MAJOR CHANGE in your life has a way of altering your social circle. For example, when people get married or have children, they find themselves connecting with more couples or more people who also have children, simply because they have more in common with them. The same is frequently true of being disabled. Especially, as in my case, when you become active as a spokesperson and fund-raiser.

Of course, as debilitating illnesses and accidents are so common, I often meet people from outside the disabled community who later, tragically, join it. In 2013 alone, my friends Stephen, Jennifer, Beth, Ginger, Peter, Ed, and Francis all suffered serious illnesses or accidents. And this is just my social circle from the Chicagoland area. If you've read this far and still think something like this could never happen to you, think again. I get chills just thinking of this list of my friends.

One of my friends, Beth, was kind enough to share with me her thoughts and the critical moments in her life journey, from her first realization that everything was going to change and that her life was never, ever going to be the same again.

It was Monday, August 5, and Beth was hailing a cab on her way to work. As she sat there, pondering her upcoming day, she started to feel a headache coming on. *Oh, great,* Beth thought. That was exactly what she needed on a morning when she was already running late.

The cab pulled up outside her office building and Beth exited, only to be hit with a sharp spike of pain that started in her head and knifed down her body. Beth's knees bent involuntarily and uncontrollable tears filled her eyes.

Slowly, she made her way over to the edge of the building and leaned heavily on it, hoping to gather herself and ride out the pain. An elderly man approached her and asked her if she needed help. By this time, the pain had started to subside, so Beth just said, "No, but thank you!"

Assuming the episode was over, Beth went about her business normally, although she did schedule a doctor's visit for the following day. After examining her, the physician prescribed a couple of headache medications and sent her on her way. They appeared to do the trick as a couple of weeks passed with no repeat of the incident.

Eventually, however, the headaches began to come back.

They were erratic and seemingly random and Beth started to suspect that the medications weren't doing anything other than making her sleepy and irritable.

She scheduled another doctor's appointment and this time she was adamant that her symptoms be examined more completely. To that end, an MRI brain scan was done and Beth was told that her results would be available in a couple of days.

A few days later, the doctor's office called to say her results were available. But that wasn't all: they suggested she bring a family member or significant other into the meeting. With a sick feeling in the pit of her stomach, Beth took her parents with her to see the doctor on August 23, 2013.

Beth's diagnosis was more serious than anyone had suspected—stage IV brain cancer. Glioblastoma multiform (GBM) is a highly aggressive and complex type of brain tumor. It is one of the most devastating forms of cancer and it affects thousands of Americans each day. And now it was growing inside Beth's brain.

Beth is only thirty-six years old. She texted me that same day, "My life has officially changed."

In her own words:

"When I was first diagnosed with brain cancer, glioblastoma stage IV, a friend of mine wanted to come visit after I had brain surgery. I told her I wasn't up for visitors—could she give me a day or two to get myself back on track? I looked as though I had been in an awful fight, with black-and-blue eyes and a bandage wrapped around my head. Her response to me was, 'This isn't just about you.'

"Beth thought, 'It's not? My brain cancer is not about me? It's about you?'

"What my friend didn't realize was that in a matter of three weeks I received a life-changing, very turbulent diagnosis. I had to give up so much so quickly that I needed to comprehend what was going on. Had I just been delivered a death sentence, or was this an illness that thirty-something-year-olds make it through? My mind was going in a million directions and throw into that my strong trait of despising confrontation. I did not know how to respond to my friend. So I didn't.

"I read an article in the *Boston Globe* in 2013 about how to handle a serious diagnosis and the people in your personal network. The article stressed that this works for all types of crises—medical, legal, financial, and romantic. It's called the Circle Theory.

"Here is the basic idea. Draw a circle. In the center of the circle, put the name of the person at the center of trauma. That's me. Next draw a circle around that one. Put the names next closest to the trauma: my parents. And go on until you have covered the closest people in your life, intimate friends, or distant relatives.

"Here is how you handle the diagram. The person in the center circle has the permission to whine, complain, and curse all day and all night how unfair life is or the why-me scenario. Everyone else can say those things but only to the people in the larger circles. The point of this is that listening is more helpful than talking. But if you are going to say something, ask yourself, is this going to provide comfort and support? People in the middle of a trauma don't need advice. They are looking for empathy and good, positive vibes.

"The point of this theory is, comfort *in*, dump *out*. Nobody would complain to the center circle as to how awful she looks. Nobody would complain that looking at the patient makes them realize their own closeness to death or life-changing disability. It teaches us not to dump into the center circle.

"As time moved on, not only did I get some of my strength back, but also my mental power, and I started speaking up on what I wanted. I thought this might be the only opportunity I had, so I might as well do something. Until something like a life-threatening illness is thrown in your direction, you don't realize the magnitude of your inner circle as to how much you want them around when it is right for you.

"Here are some other things I am learning while I am on my personal journey:

"I will inspire others. It will feel weird.

"When you get to the other side, you won't believe it. They will tell you the disease is gone. Everyone is celebrating and returning back to their lives. The greatest gift you've been given is that you're going to make the most of every second. How you see the world moving forward will become more clear.

"You will feel fear. The people who love you are just as scared as you are.

"I was diagnosed with brain cancer in October 2013. I had brain surgery a week later. I am currently receiving chemotherapy treatments for the next twelve to fourteen months. And I am extremely grateful for the people in my life and they know it."

As a result of her diagnosis, Beth was able to connect with Imerman Angels (for more about this group, see page 100) a network of people who have been affected by cancer either as fighters, survivors, or caregivers. It enables people who are living with this disease to get involved in one another's lives and offer critical support from the perspective of someone who has had similar experiences.

This brings up the elephant in the room when it comes to illness or disability: charity. For thousands of years, sick and disabled individuals have had little recourse except to depend on, as Blanche DuBois famously said, the kindness of strangers. Society has developed a number of other options for people to prepare for these kinds of eventualities, but there is also a whole host of new ways to give—and receive.

If you're anything like me, you get any number of donation requests from friends and acquaintances each year, generally via e-mail or social media. These requests tend to fall into two categories: requests for donations from an organization, association, or charity that advocates for a certain cause from cancer to natural disasters; or calls to contribute to an individual who has suffered an accident or illness and needs help covering medical, living, and other expenses.

This brings me to the story of Rachelle Friedman. I met Rachelle through our shared involvement in the larger community of folks who have suffered spinal cord injuries. Rachelle was paralyzed during her bachelorette party when she was pushed into the shallow end of a swimming pool, damaging her spine. Since her accident, she has become one of the most visible speakers, commentators, and ambassadors for the spinal cord injury community.

She wrote an article for the Huffington Post entitled "8 Misconceptions About Life With Paralysis," in which she dissects the limitations of medical insurance when it comes to providing for whole-person care.

"Many daily items are considered luxury items and are not covered [by medical insurance]," Rachelle wrote. "This includes shower chairs, lightweight wheelchairs, and other adapted equipment. And of course insurance doesn't cover home modifications and adapted vehicles. My driving evaluation was over

$1,000 alone. [Medical insurance] pretty much covers the bare minimum."[11]

Most of us have no idea how many small costs contribute to the overall financial need of a person who is disabled. It's no wonder that people often have to reach out to the larger community when they run up against these unanticipated expenses.

As you know from my story, I raise money for both causes and people. The personal stories behind these calls for aid are heartbreaking and the causes are certainly important. I am not convinced, however, that the charity model is the best solution to the problem of how to manage the terrible expense of living with a disability. Plus, while we regularly donate to others, we rarely think about contributing to our own personal causes. If you could donate to yourself, to the protection of your ability to earn a living, would you do it? As my mother always said: charity begins at home.

This is not, by any means, meant to discount the importance of giving to others. There are few among us who have never been touched by an accident or illness. Almost all of us have family, friends, neighbors, coworkers, or peers who have suffered in this way. As humans, we are all interconnected and we all lean on others at some point. We are all in this together.

However, if we were to place the methods of coping with

11 http://www.huffingtonpost.com/rachelle-friedman/misconceptions-about-paralysis_b_4644588.html?utm_hp_ref=fb&src=sp&comm_ref=false.

disability on a spectrum from "offers the most control" to "offers the least control," relying upon charity would definitely be at the latter end. You will never be able to control the amount of money that results from charitable drives—or where that money comes from and whether it has strings attached. Similarly, you have to get out there and drum up support for your cause. I have seen firsthand how raising awareness of a person or a problem can become a full-time job. Will you have the energy, capability, and network for that when you are sick or injured?

• • •

Accidents and illnesses do not discriminate. They can and do happen to people from all walks of life.

In January of 2012, Illinois senator Mark Kirk suffered a stroke. His physicians expect that he will need to deal with long-term physical impairments, though not cognitive ones. Since the stroke, he has become a vocal proponent of the value of disability insurance and back-to-work benefits in terms of securing our financial foundations. Right now he is leading a caucus on the topic to raise awareness—the Congressional Income Protection Caucus. See Appendix B, at the back of the book, for the Congressional Income Protection Caucus Fact Sheet.

"Many Americans have insurance for their pets and cell phones and nearly all have insurance on their homes and cars," said a letter cosigned by Kirk and three other lawmakers leading the caucus. "Yet too few Americans—roughly only one-third—have insurance on their most valuable asset: their ability to earn an income."[12]

Part of the goal is shifting the burden of providing for disability onto private disability insurance providers and away from the Disability Insurance Trust Fund—which is currently set to run dry by 2016. For the past four years in a row, debits against the fund have surpassed credits—a historically unprecedented occurrence.

The problem with the fund is that there are simply too many disabled Americans to cover. Remember our tendency to imagine it couldn't happen to us? Well, it's happening to so many of us that there are now only thirteen Americans working full-time for each worker on disability. For comparison, in 1968, that rate was more like fifty workers per person on disability.

It is fashionable to blame these statistics on spurious disabled claims or expanding definitions of disability. However, it's not as though Americans drawing disability are living in the lap of luxury. With the average monthly payment barely

12 http://insurancenewsnet.com/innarticle/2013/10/31/lawmakers-launch-disability-income-protection-caucus-a-413678.html#.UxzeK8KYbzB.

clearing $1,000, many disabled Americans can't even afford to rent a one-bedroom apartment in many major cities.

Supplementing a taxpayer-financed disability paycheck through a private policy is a better private-sector option, according to Sen. Kirk's caucus. A disability policy offered through an employer costs an average of $300 a year and saves taxpayers $4.5 billion a year in disability payments, payments that the government and taxpayers otherwise would have to fund.

"Disability income insurers—indeed, all insurers—augment the public safety net,"[13] said Dirk Kempthorne, president and chief executive officer of the American Council of Life Insurers, in a news release, agreeing with the creation of the Congressional Income Protection Caucus.

• • •

Jim Cramer is on top of the financial world, with his own show on CNBC, where he dishes out daily stock picks for his massive audience.

Recently, he spoke out on strategies for preserving your investment capital and he was right on the money. His advice must have resonated with people, because his report was the number-five trending business and investing story on social media in February 2014.

13 http://insurancenewsnet.com/innarticle/2013/10/31/lawmakers-launch-disability-income-protection-caucus-a-413678.html#.UxzeK8KYbzB.

Cramer's strategies are simple, straightforward, and applicable to all of us. Regardless of your level of expertise and experience, whether or not you invest your money, there is something valuable to glean from these tips. Personally, I believe that these strategies go way beyond just preserving your investment capital. They are basic financial foundational strategies that we all need to implement to secure our livelihoods.

1. Pay off your credit card debt—this is a straightforward risk/reward strategy.
2. Own health insurance—don't let a single sickness or injury financially wipe you.
3. Own disability insurance—protect your ability to earn an income.[14]

These may seem like basic tips—even common sense. Yet every day I hear a steady stream of excuses and reasons from people about why they can't and don't obtain disability insurance. Some of the most common are:

"I'm familiar with the products and the information is clear enough—I just have to evaluate any changes within my life now or the near future and decide on appropriate benefits."

This sounds reasonable enough, on the face of it. However, as we saw before with the urgent/important exercise, people

14 http://www.fool.com/investing/general/2014/02/27/jim-cramer-finally-gets-it-right.aspx.

will put off the things that don't immediately demand your attention. The longer you wait before buying the products, the greater your chances of suffering an accident or illness. Don't wait until your back is against the wall to protect yourself.

"I don't really know how to evaluate the various products other than price. I might feel dumb to ask. It seems so complicated and I'm overwhelmed by the information."

Again, this is a seemingly reasonable objection that doesn't really hold up to scrutiny. To go back to our parachute idea, would anyone ever say, "There are too many types of parachutes! I'm afraid to ask how to fold them! Why don't I just jump and hope for the best?"

"I'm tired of spending time on projecting future possibilities I can't predict. I don't have time or energy—I almost just don't care. It is easier to not do anything."

This is possibly the hardest objection to counter because it is rooted in delusion and avoidance. People who don't see any value in thinking about the future are fundamentally self-deluding. All I can really say to this kind of objection is that not caring about disability insurance is tantamount to not caring about your physical, emotional, and mental health. It's tantamount to not caring about your dependents (spouse, children, family). It's tantamount to not caring about your income or your financial future. It's tantamount to not caring about your goals, hopes, and dreams.

To put it another way, consider the stock market. It has been said that we are entering into the era of an investing society—the role of stock market is increasingly central to our money, business, and economy.

There is a critical concept in investing called the stop loss. Stop loss is a market order to sell a security if its value sinks to a previously specified price; this is intended to limit loss. Naturally, I'm a big fan of the stop loss system, because I never buy a stock without protecting against downside risk.

As an investor, you have to make a decision about where you place your stop loss price. The S&P 500 stock chart below shows the past five years of market performance. As you can see, we have been in a bull market with great market price gains. So where would you place your stop loss? How much of those gains do you want to protect?

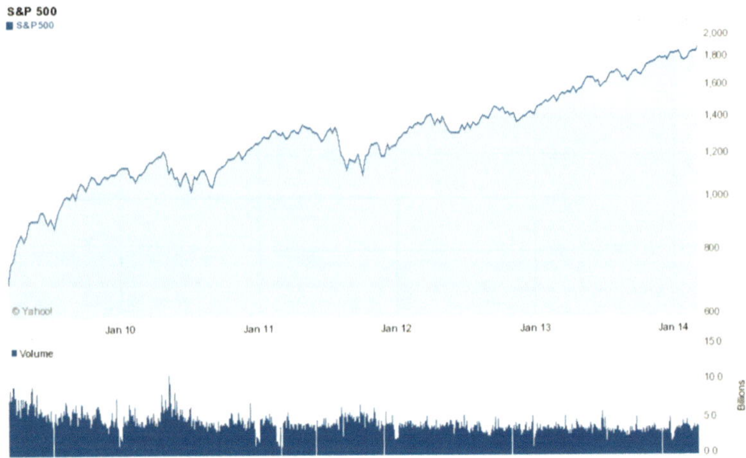

One of my favorite stock investments of late has been DDD 3-D printing company. It has been rising quickly, going from $30 per share to over $90 per share within a year. That is a fantastic paper gain. Intelligent investors protect these gains and thus their ability to capture more gains in the future, and so I set my own stop loss at $87 per share for this particular stock.

This exact same concept applies to your talents and your abilities to earn an income. Your ability to earn income is like the shares of a profitable stock—you have long-term potential and an increasing valuation. Disability insurance is your stop loss strategy that will protect you from the downside potential and provide income in the event you have a loss of ability to perform your work. In the case of DDD 3-D printing, the difference between $90 per share and $87 was analogous to the deductible. After that, the profits were all mine.

If you don't take steps to protect yourself in the stock market, investing becomes nothing more than gambling. Similarly, if you choose not to protect your mental, physical, and emotional capital and your ability to earn income, you are also gambling, but with something infinitely more important: your life and the lives of those you love.

CHAPTER 9

The Final Word — Let's Hope Not

IN THE WORDS of Nike, just do it. Learn, ask, and decide to take action. Empower yourself with knowledge so you can make an informed decision. Ignoring is easy and you will always be able to say, "I didn't know what I didn't know." However, now you know. Let that be the spark to take the next steps.

Leaders lead and the first step is leadership of self. In Albert Gray's speech entitled "The Common Denominator of Success," he states that the secret of success lies in the fact that successful people form the habit of doing the things that failures don't like to do.

Why are successful people able to do the things unsuccessful people do not like to do? Successful people have a purpose strong enough to make them form the habits so they can accomplish their purpose—their mission in life.

My habit of personal responsibility led to the decision to protect my talents and the abilities that create my income. Disability insurance benefits protected my purpose. My purpose of serving others with all my heart, mind, and resources remains intact, centered, and even enhanced by a multiple of one hundred. That is the power of disability insurance in the event of a disabling accident or illness.

Maybe it should be called purpose insurance. The choice is yours.

Balance Sheet of Your Name Inc.

ASSETS	LIABILITIES
Bank accounts	Debts
Toys/Valuables	Mortgage
House	Credit cards
Stocks and bonds	Student loans
Cars	
Pension	
Total: **$_________**	**Total:** **$_________**
+ **HUMAN CAPITAL $_________**	
Net Worth Grand Total $ _________	

Note: HUMAN CAPITAL is converted to financial capital as you age.

Assets + HUMAN CAPITAL – Debts and Liabilities = Net Worth

Congressional Income Protection Caucus Fact Sheet

Workplace disability insurance benefits provide individuals and families with financial security to better cope with the inability to work due to illness or injury. Most people have neither the savings nor insurance protection to provide for themselves or their families should a life-changing event occur. Disability benefits pay a portion of an individual's salary while he or she is unable to work.

Many middle- and lower-income Americans are ill prepared for the financial impact of injury or illness.

More than three-quarters (77 percent) of workers think that missing work for three months because of injury or illness would create a financial hardship.

Half of Americans have less than $10,000 in savings.

Yet many Americans will likely face loss of income due to these events.

The Social Security Administration estimates that just over one in four of today's twenty-year-olds will become disabled before reaching age sixty-seven.

Approximately 90 percent of all disabilities are caused by illnesses rather than accidents.

Government safety net programs face funding and budgetary pressures.

Current government safety net programs are insufficient to address all the financial needs of disabled Americans. Such programs are difficult to expand given current budgetary pressures.

Engaging the private sector is key to addressing America's strained safety net. Income protection benefits offer assistance to vulnerable workers and their families. If all workers were covered by standard employer-sponsored insurance, poverty arising from work disability would be virtually eliminated. Yet 67 percent of private sector workers do not have access to employer-sponsored long-term disability insurance.

The workplace is an ideal setting to educate Americans about benefit options and the steps they can take to protect their families. Employers not only provide access to benefits, they also offer education and support that allow Americans to choose benefits that can most effectively protect their lifestyle and financial security.

Nearly three-quarters of employees (72 percent) who indicated that they knew "a little" or "a lot" about disability insurance cited their present or past employer as their principal information source.

Once employees learn about disability insurance, the vast majority recognize its value:

- 90 percent of employees think employers should make this insurance available to their employees.
- 88 percent of employees think it is important for them personally to be covered.

Consumer Federation of America and Unum, Employee Knowledge and Attitudes about Employer-Provided Disability Insurance (2012).

US Senate Committee on Health, Education, Labor & Pensions, The Retirement Crisis and a Plan to Solve It (2012).

Social Security Administration, "Basic Facts" (Feb. 7, 2013; accessed March 20, 2013), http://www.ssa.gov/pressoffice/basicfact.htm.

Council for Disability Awareness, "Chances of Disability: Me, Disabled?" (2012; accessed Oct. 29, 2012), http://www.disabilitycanhappen.org/chances_disability/disability_stats.asp.

Charles River Associates (prepared for Unum), Financial Security for Working Americans: An Economic Analysis of Insurance Products in Workplace Benefits Programs (2011).

Bureau of Labor Statistics, "National Compensation Survey: Employee Benefits in the United States, March 2012" (accessed Oct. 29, 2012), http://www.bls.gov/ncs/ebs/benefits/2012/ownership/private/table12a.pdf.

Consumer Federation of America and Unum, Employee Knowledge and Attitudes about Employer-Provided Disability Insurance (2012).

Consumer Federation of America and Unum, Employee Knowledge and Attitudes about Employer-Provided Disability Insurance (2012).

The Reverse Lottery and the Money Box

Another cool friend of mine, Maria Ferrante-Schepis, created a couple of videos that share a perspective on sharing and giving that fits into the topic of insurance. Check out:

"The Reverse Lottery"
http://flirtingwiththeuninterested.com/the-reverse-lottery/

The second video speaks to how insurance works and is entitled:

"The Money Box"
http://flirtingwiththeuninterested.com/themoneybox/

——

Maria Ferrante-Schepis, Managing Principal
— Insurance & Financial Services Innovation

Maddock Douglas, Empower Next
www.maddockdouglas.com

maria.fs@maddockdouglas.com
Direct: 630-563-6487

Imerman Angels

Providing Personalized Connections that Enable One-on-One Support among Cancer Fighters, Survivors, and Caregivers

CHICAGO (February 2014)—Imerman Angels provides personalized connections that enable one-on-one support among cancer fighters, survivors, and caregivers. The 501(c)(3) not-for-profit organization carefully matches and individually pairs a person touched by cancer (a cancer fighter) with someone who has fought and survived the same type of cancer (a mentor angel). A mentor angel is walking, talking, living proof and inspiration that cancer can be beaten.

Cancer caregivers (spouses, parents, children, and other family and friends of fighters) also receive one-on-one connections with other caregivers and survivors.

These one-on-one relationships give a cancer fighter or caregiver the chance to ask personal questions and get support from someone who has been there before. Mentor angels can lend support and empathy and help cancer fighters and caregivers navigate the system, determine their options, and create their own support systems. Frequently, caregivers experience feelings similar to those of the person facing cancer. Mentor angels can relate while being sensitive to the experience and situation.

Today, Imerman Angels has the largest database of cancer fighters and survivors in the world. The service is absolutely free and helps anyone touched by any type of cancer, at any cancer stage level, at any age, living anywhere across the globe.

Imerman Angels is a federally registered 501(c)(3) not-for-profit organization. Visit **www.ImermanAngels.org** for information on how to support or join the network of cancer fighters, survivors, and caregivers.

The Spine Health Foundation, Inc. (SHF)

Founded in 2010, the Spine Health Foundation Inc. (SHF) is making an impact in the lives of people who suffer from chronic pain related to untreated spinal injuries or disorders.

Our participating physicians and generous donors have been vital in helping SHF fulfill our mission of helping disadvantaged individuals gain access to specialized spine care, psychological resources, and education. Since February 2011, SHF has provided individuals with over three hundred medically related resources, including seventeen spine surgeries.

For the working wounded who are uninsured or underinsured and suffer with chronic pain related to a spinal disorder, accessing specialized spine care can be financially out of reach. SHF was created to fill an unmet health care need by providing access to appropriate specialized spine care for the uninsured or disadvantaged.

The goals of SHF are to help the whole person regain their health and get back to life, work, and family. Untreated spinal disorders or injuries can lead to chronic depression, pain medication addiction, family breakdown, paralysis, and even suicide. Other SHF resources include psychological support and education. SHF is dedicated to providing hope and healing solutions to those in need.

In May 2013, Jim was exhausted, with constant pain stemming from an untreated spinal condition. Uninsured and unable to afford to consult with a spine specialist, he was taken to a local ER by his family. The ER staff recognized the severity of Jim's condition and sent him on to Johnson City Medical Center (JCMC) to be evaluated by the neurosurgeon on duty. By this time, Jim's pain had persisted for months, becoming worse each day. The constant "electric-like" pain he was feeling was diagnosed as lumbar intervertebral disc displacement with neuritis.

Jim continued to work each day even though he experienced continuous chronic pain, not knowing if he would ever overcome the pain and regain the health he once knew. Fortunately, the neurosurgeon on duty was a participating provider of the SHF. The physician recognized the need for Jim to have spine surgery, but also understood he was uninsured. Jim was referred to the Spine Health Foundation and was approved for assistance. He was able to continue his appointments with his neurosurgeon without interruption and scheduled his spine surgery in July 2013. Prior to the surgery, Jim's pain level was ten (ten being the worst). After the surgery, Jim's pain level dropped to zero.

Jim follows his physician's instructions to protect and care for his spine, and has returned to work to support his family. "I am thankful to God and for the SHF for what they've done to help me," Jim says. "Before the SHF stepped in, I was slowing losing my will to survive...giving up hope that I would ever be free of constant pain. Now I have another chance at my future."

For more information, visit:
www.spinehealthfoundation.org

WHEELSTRONG SPORTS

The company's mission statement says it all:

"We at Wheelstrong Sports want to unite athletes of adaptive sports into the Wheelstrong community. Our goal is to inspire, motivate, encourage, support, innovate, and give back to others of all levels and capabilities to help accomplish their goals."

According to Matthew Celeberto, founder of Wheelstrong Sports, "We are preparing to change adaptive sports and fitness forever, to inspire and support wheelchair athletes. Before we came along, athletes in the adaptive sports community were wearing brands like Nike or Adidas. I decided that we needed our own clothing line—a brand that would inspire us and show the world how strong and competitive we are."

To this end, Wheelstrong Sports is adding a new line of clothing, backpacks, and wheelchair accessories to its line of apparel for the adaptive athletics and fitness community. The company also maintains an online support network for the adaptive sports and fitness community. The website provides visitors with a place to learn about fitness and support each other. It also features weekly fitness and workout videos, downloadable fitness eBooks, and the ability for visitors to communicate in Google+ Hangouts to discuss athletics and fitness.

"Our tagline is 'Only for the strong,'" Celeberto explains. "It's important for athletes in wheelchairs to believe in their strengths and reach beyond their limitations. It's also important for the world to see that we can train and compete at high levels."

Celeberto became a T8 paraplegic after suffering a severe spinal cord injury in a 2003 auto accident. But being in a wheelchair would not keep Celeberto away from his love of fitness and sports. Having grown up lifting weights and playing hockey and football, Celeberto founded Wheelstrong Sports to be a champion for wheelchair fitness and sports.

To learn more, visit www.wheelstrong.com or contact Matthew Celeberto at (401) 305-4541, ext. 1. You can also e-mail Matthew at **matt@wheelstrong.com**.

John F. Nichols, MSM, CLU
Here to serve.

---

jfn@drdgi.com
www.johnfnichols.com